THE BOOK OF WRONG

The Book of Wrong

A Silly Look at History and the Not-So-Serious People Who May (or May Not) Have Made It

Steven Hawkins

Willow Grove Publishers

Mea navis aëricumbens anguillis abundant.

CONTENTS

1

GAIUS JULIUS CAESAR

LEAVE THE SWORD; TAKE THE CANNOLI

The tall, lanky redheaded man stood upon a marble bench and looked out at the group of XII people filling the atrium before him, the bright Mediterranean sun beating down upon their tanned bodies, every person weary from the long, just-completed journey. He smiled and tried to look as friendly and reassuring as he could, making sure he made eye contact with each one to instill trust.

"Greetings one and all. And welcome to your new home. I assume you have each picked up a significant amount of Latin while on your journeys, so you should all be able to understand me at this point. There are, of course, colloquialisms in your new land of Roma that you will probably hear from time-to-time such as, 'What? You think you're better than me?' 'Whatsa matta wit you?' And 'Would ya just watch the hair? Don't toucha my hair!' But for now, Latin will suffice."

Most in the crowd nodded. They understood—they were not terribly happy about their current predicament, but they understood.

"Fabulous. Fabulous. Well, I must say, you all look wonderful after your long trip. I can already feel the fantastic enthusiasm and energy emanating from you for the upcoming projects here. And I for one am super, super excited about the potential each and every one of you brings here."

A slight, painful groan rose from the group.

"My name is Bodiccius. I am originally from a northern realm called Briton. Any Britons out there?" He stroked his bushy beard and scanned the people but did not see any hands raised. "Oh well, that's all right. My name in my land means 'He who is a great victor.' Ironic, huh, since I was captured the same as all of you and sent here many years ago."

A handful of people snorted nervously in agreement.

"So you are a slave too?" a muscular, shaggy man from the back called out.

"Shhh," Bodiccius quickly replied, his eyes scanning to see if anyone had heard. "We do not use that word here. It is frowned upon greatly. No, the preferred term is 'people who work in exchange for food, clothing, and shelter.'"

"That's a mouthful in any language," a woman's voice with a Frankish accent called out. "So what is your job?

Are you the top sla . . . I mean, person who works in exchange for . . . stuff?"

"That is an excellent question, madam." Bodiccius stood tall and straightened out his toga. "I happen to be the director of human resources in charge of all of you."

"The direct what?" the withered, elderly woman asked.

The muscular, shaggy man leaned down and whispered to her, "He's the head slave."

"Ah," she said before calling out, "but what does that mean exactly?"

"I use my many years of expertise to assign you suitable positions that match your skillset. For instance, madam, excuse me. What is your name and what talents do you have?"

"Sylvie, and I cook."

"Splendid, Sylvie," replied Bodiccius, repeating her name so that he would more easily remember it. "Then I shall probably assign you to the kitchen. Hopefully, you will introduce some exotic new dishes to the household from your former homeland."

"There is one you might like. We call it '*escargot*.'"

"Marvelous, Sylvie," the human resources director exclaimed. "And what is that?"

"Cooked snails."

The entire group erupted and various voices called out, "Ewwwwww. Snails?" "Seriously?" "Your people actually eat that?" "It's no wonder you lost."

The ancient, wrinkled woman looked around and mumbled, "It tastes much better than it sounds."

"That's fine," Bodiccius replied, hiding his personal disgust and using his reassuring human resources voice. "There are no bad suggestions here. We shall simply have you run the dish past the head chef first to see if she approves."

"I also make a wonderful salad," Sylvie added.

Again, Bodiccius quickly calmed himself before replying. "Yes. Yes. About that. We call them 'greens' here. We try not to use the word 'salad.'"

"Why not?" the perplexed old woman asked.

Bodiccius raised his head and looked over the group of people who work in exchange for food, clothing, and shelter. "Very well. It is time for all of you to know. You are very fortunate. You all work for the esteemed household of Julius Caesar." He then looked down to Sylvie. "And he is teased constantly by his friend Brutus about some salad being named for him. So we just go with 'greens' instead of using that word. It makes life simpler for all of us."

"Our master is Julius Caesar?" an awed voice called out. "THE Julius Caesar?"

"The one and the same," a smiling Bodiccius answered proudly. "But again, we frown upon the word 'master' and the connotations it has. So we go with a more informal, local title of respect and call him 'Don Caesar.'"

"I have a kinsman named 'Don,'" a voice from the back mentioned.

"Not the same thing," Bodiccius pointed out in response. "Now, back to the orientation."

"Orient? I thought we were in Rome," another person who works in exchange for food, clothing, and shelter called out.

Starting to get frustrated, Bodiccius took a deep breath. "We are in Roma. And when in Roma, we do as the Romans do and tackle the task at hand." He looked at the people to see if anyone was planning to interrupt. "Good. Now, let us figure out your jobs here. Is anyone a skilled craftsman?"

"Or craftswoman," Sylvie mumbled. "Let's see you make snails edible."

An elderly man raised his hand and said, "I was a coppersmith in my home in Winnili."

"Excellent!" a visibly brightened Bodiccius exclaimed. "Excellent. That always comes in handy. Well, you just move over here to my left. Sylvie, you move over to my right." They both complied. "Now, who else? Any other craftsmen?"

No one responded.

"Pity," he said. He then looked at others individually. "How about you?" he asked a filthy rag-covered man.

"Farmer."

"Ah, and you?" he asked the next disheveled man.

"Farmer."

"Well, we always need those. To my right. Both of you." He then asked the next man, "And you?"

"Village idiot."

He shrugged. "I had to ask. We'll see if we can find a position for you in the Senate." The human resources director next looked at the muscular, shaggy man standing in the back of the group. "And you, good sir. What did you previously do?

"I am a Vandal warrior! My specialty is disembowelments."

"Splendid. Splendid," a smiling Bodiccius responded, his enthusiasm restored. "We have the perfect job that has just opened up for a warrior of your strength and perseverance." He paused for effect. "You shall clean the manure from Don Caesar's stables."

"Clean manure! This is an insult!"

"Oh no, no, no," the polite Brit replied. "It is, in fact, a great honor. The mighty Caesar loves his horses. And if you do a good job, in five years or so . . . ."

"I shall be granted my freedom?"

"No, you shall be issued a shovel."

"Can't I have a better job? Like in the main house?" the Vandal inquired.

"Oh, I'm afraid that is not possible. We never allow soldiers of a conquered people to work inside the house. You see, they sometimes decide they would like to stab every member of the family in revenge, pillage the villa, and then try to escape back to their homeland. If you do that, it will reflect very poorly on your annual job performance evaluation. Believe me, it is for your own good. Besides, you might find you enjoy the stables once you get used to the smell and thousands of flies biting you."

He turned his attention back to the people and said, "Now. Clothing. We shall burn those filthy rags you are wearing and issue each of you a clean toga."

"Togas?" the village idiot asked. "I have heard of wild Roman toga parties."

"Everyone here wears togas. Therefore, they do not call them 'toga parties.' They just call them 'parties.'"

"But they are still 'wild,'" the idiot offered.

"I wouldn't know," an indignant Bodiccius replied. "I have never been invited to one." He then looked around. "That reminds me. Speaking of parties. Any prostitutes in the group? Prostitutes? Anyone?" he asked, glancing sideways to make sure the weathered Sylvie did not respond.

No one raised a hand, although the Vandal warrior briefly considered doing so if it meant work in the villa rather than the stables. In the end, his hand remained at his side.

"Never mind. I am always required to ask, just in case. Apparently, you can never have enough on your staff."

Suddenly a voice accustomed to command boomed out from behind him, "Bodiccius! Are you asking for the household or for yourself?" He then laughed loudly at his own joke.

"Don Caesar!" the man cried out as he jumped off the bench and bowed low before Gaius Julius Caesar. "I was not expecting you back from inspecting the spring plantings in the southern fields so soon."

"I did not go. The stables are a mess. An entire legion of flies kept me at bay."

Bodiccius looked over at the Vandal and raised his eyebrow in a knowing fashion.

The regal, formidable Caesar turned to the group, placed his hand upon his Roman short sword and asked, "So, are these the people who work in exchange for food, clothing, and shelter?"

"They are, Don Caesar."

"Good. Good." He then turned to the group. "Friends. New Romans. Country folk. Lend me your ears."

They looked at their new master, despite his title, with guarded suspicion.

"I know many of you are frightened and worried about your new lives, but you need not be. Roma is a great place to be. It is growing at a fantastic pace. I am pretty sure we are going to be an empire in the very near future. And that is a good thing for all. Our gods are already supplanting the Greek gods. And I certainly don't see any god coming along in the near future to push ours out of the way. Plus, wherever we go, we build. Aqueducts. Hot baths. Roads from one end of the known world to the other." He then motioned to Bodiccius. "Even in Briton, we have constructed roads to link all corners of his accursed damp island. Although, for some inexplicable reason, the bloody Brits insist on driving their carts on the wrong side of these roads."

Sylvie and the others nodded their heads politely.

"Very inspiring, Don Caesar. Very inspiring," the eager-to-please Brit stepped in to say.

"Oh, and while I am thinking about it, Bodiccius. You need to have a sumptuous feast prepared for this evening. Don Brutus, Don Labeo, Don Cassius, and Don Mark Antony are coming over."

"So the heads of the five families will all be here?"

"Yes," he replied.

"Then as you wish, Don Caesar."

"And Bodiccius," he added. "Remember, no greens tonight. Brutus loves sticking it to me about my name."

"Kale, Caesar?"

"Not even that," he dismissed with a wave of his hand. "Now I am going to lie down for a while. I have had a stabbing pain in the chest all day."

I'm sure it is nothing," the accommodating Bodiccius replied. "It will pass into history."

"As will I. As will I," mumbled Gaius Julius Caesar. "But not for a very long time, I am sure. The ides are against it."

"Odds," Bodiccius corrected him.

"Ides. Odds. It will all be good in the end."

"I am sure it will be," Bodiccius said with a deep bow. "Your life shall be filled with *Pax Romana*, I pray to your gods."

The powerful general then turned back to the people who work in exchange for food, clothing, and shelter. "One more thing I should add before I leave you this day. I know many of you are thinking about it. You could *try* to escape back to your homelands, but it is a very long and arduous way. You would be captured and then crucified. And, let me tell you, if you don't know what crucifixion is, you are better off not knowing. It is extremely painful and bloody and awful. Better that you should work here for me rather than to have to deal with such unfortunate, violent consequences." He stopped and stroked the bottom of neck with the back with his left hand while firmly grasping his sword with his right. "I am making you an offer you can't refuse."

2

LEIF ERIKSON

COLUMBUS CAN EAT MY DUST

The shivering herald pushed through the fur-covered entryway, approached his master sitting upon the throne in the great hall, and bowed. "My lord, there is someone here requesting an audience."

The older gentlemen adjusted the fur around his shoulder as a cold rush of wind followed his servant through the entrance and replied, "I'm not really in the mood today to receive visitors. Can't we just tell him I'm out on a raid or something?"

"I am sorry, my monotonous lord," the herald replied, bowing even lower. "But he is a kinsman to you. Protocol says you must see him."

"Kinsman? How?"

"He is your second cousin twice removed," the herald answered.

"That's the problem with Vikings and Iceland. We all intermarry so much that we are all related to each other somehow. So I end up having to see every Torbjorg, Dag, or Hagrid that comes along." He tried to get more comfortable in his chair before saying, "Very well. Send whoever it is in."

The herald rose and rushed through the door covering to summon the awaiting visitor before scurrying back to the side of his sullen master.

In strode a tall, handsome man with a flowing robe and a slightly smaller, muscular gruff-looking man.

"King Olaf Tryggvason," the man's voice boomed as he put his right hand to his heart and bowed ever so slightly. "I am Leif Erikson. Son of Erik the Red."

The old king nodded in reply. "Oh, ja. Now I remember you. You are the one who discovered that accursed Greenland. And who is this also with you?"

Leif thrust an arm in the direction of the other Viking. "This is my companion, Erik the Blondish Red with Flecks of Gray."

King Olaf leaned over and whispered to his nearby herald, "Make a note, we have got to do something about some of these silly names people are running around with."

The herald nodded in fervent agreement.

"So why are you here, young Erikson? Why have you and Erik the Blond . . . Fuzzy . . . Whatever . . . requested an audience?"

"My good king, we have been gone for many months because we have had a happy accident while on our way to our Greenland villages. A great storm blew us farther west than any Viking has ever sailed, and we have discovered a wonderful new land."

"A great storm, you say? Isn't that how you discovered Greenland a while back?"

"Actually, good King," Erik the Blondish Red with Gray Flecks interrupted. "It wasn't really a storm that got us there. Truth be told be told, we had a little too much to drink one night and then SOMEBODY—and I'm not naming names here." He nodded his head sideways at Leif. "SOMEBODY decided they could steer by the stars while drunk. And that's how we got so far off course."

King Olaf raised an eyebrow and nodded. "Ja, we have all been there. Done that."

"WHATEVER the reason," Erikson butted back in, "we discovered a new and wondrous land far, far to the west of anywhere we have ever been. Much farther than any of the European ships' captains have ever dared go."

"Although I am sure when they do, they will claim they were the first. They always do," the herald said to himself. "We really should write some of this stuff down and take credit for it."

The Viking king ignored his bitter aide's grousing and inquired, "Better than frigid Greenland? The only land on the planet that makes our old home in Norway seem tepid."

"Much, much better, astute King Olaf. We even brought back grapes and timber from this new land to show you. Two things Greenland is sorely lacking."

"Well, truth be told, the grapes didn't really make it all the way back," mumbled Erik the Blondish Red with Flecks of Gray. "But they were yummy!"

The old king nodded and said, "Very well. Sounds promising. So what have you named this land?"

"Vinland, wise King Olaf."

"Vinland? As in Wineland? Nei. Nei. Nei. Are you insane? You are telling all the world of its most-promising asset. Look, we named this place Iceland because the weather is fairly decent, and we don't want any other realms interested in wanting to come and take it from us. We only named Greenland that because it is the most miserable place in the discovered world, and we are hoping to unload it on some unsuspecting monarch looking for some fixer-upper real estate." The king took a deep breath before adding, "If it gets out we are calling it Vinland, every drunk Irishman with a currach will come paddling over to get away from their pious priests."

"Then what would you suggest we call this newly found land, my prudent king?"

King Olaf threw up his hands and let out a deep breath. "I don't know. It should probably be something generic, not very exciting. Something that won't attract the interest of the known world."

"How about New Found Land?" mumbled Erik the Blondish Red with Flecks of Gray.

King Olaf brightened. He snapped his fingers and declared, "I have it. We'll call it Newfoundland."

"Brilliant, my lactating lord," his cowering herald stated a little too loudly because he had been dozing off.

King Olaf Tryggvason nodded his agreement to his herald before turning back to the two Viking explorers before him. "If this land is so good and full of plenty, are there native tribes already living there?"

"Yes, my sagacious king, "Leif answered. "But they are of no consequence. They have crude weapons that are no match to our shields, swords, and axes."

The king stared at his ambitious, distant kinsman before asking, "Are they Inuit? The Inuit in Greenland also have only crude weapons, but they seem to be able to kick our rumpes up one side of the island and down the other. And we're VIKINGS!"

"They are called the Beothuk, my shrewd king, but we discovered something astounding about them. We interacted with them a few times. But one time, one of my drengr, called Orm the One Green Eye, the Other Blue Eye with a Cowlick, came down with a cold while we were trading with the tribe." King Olaf and his herald gave each other a knowing glance over the name. "The next day, several of their tribe came down sick with a cold, and a week later, one quarter of them were dead."

"Really!" King Olaf exclaimed. "Is this true?"

"It is, my erudite king."

“I mean, it is much more impressive if we could simply slay them all in battle Viking style with an axe through a skull, but if they simply get the sniffles and die off, leaving us the land, then so be it.” He then pounded the arm of his chair. “Very well, then. Leif Erikson, I command you to return to this Newfoundland and establish a permanent Viking colony.”

“Oooo, I would love to, my clever king, but my schedule is really booked for the next year or two. I am busy trying to Christianize those Inuits in Greenland, and those that refuse, I need to slaughter. I am currently overwhelmed.”

The Viking king pointed to Leif Erikson’s companion. “Well, what about Erik the Blond Pink-Haired Bad Dye Job? Perhaps he can go in your stead.”

“I would be honored, King Gustav,” Erik the Blondish Red with Flecks of Gray answered with a bow.

“That’s Olaf,” the king corrected him.

“I know,” Erik the Blondish Red with Flecks of Gray mumbled too softly for his monarch to hear.

“Then it is settled. Herald, take note of what was said here today. Erik the Reddish Brown with Flecks of White shall be the one to go and bring honor to the Viking people.”

“But oblivious King Olaf,” the herald whispered to him. “There is no way I nor anyone else is going to remember that long, incomprehensible last name.”

The king whispered back to him, “Very well. Just give all the credit for the discovery and first settlement at

Newfoundland to Leif Erikson then. That's an easy name for folks to sing songs about at feasts."

"But what of the surviving Beothuk tribe? Are we to go ahead and kill them as soon as we arrive, my fatuous king?" Erik the Blondish Red with Flecks of Gray inquired.

"Nei. Wait until you have established a colony and they have taught you the ways of the land there and if there are any other valuables to be gleaned from this Newfoundland—then slaughter them and take all the surrounding territory in my name."

"As you wish, my tedious king," he replied.

And with that, Erik the Blondish Red with Flecks of Gray assembled a crew and set off for Newfoundland and established a small, Viking colony, interacting with the Beothuk people, and learning their ways until two months later in the middle of one night when the warriors of the tribe snuck into their camp and killed all of the Vikings as revenge for introducing them to the common cold and because they could never remember the long Viking names.

3

SIR FRANCIS BACON

TIS SIR WILLIAM FRANCIS SHAKESPEARE BACON

Slowly the heavy door creaked opened as the servant slid in as quietly as he could. Standing silently, he watched his master, quill in hand, write at a feverish pace. He waited until the quill had ceased moving across the paper before he spoke.

"Sir Francis?"

The gentleman looked up from his desk and glared at his longtime servant. "Cedric, thou can see that I am working. What have I told thee to calleth me when I have the muse upon my most creative nature?"

Cedric fought every urge in his body to roll his eyes and scream out his master's real name, "Sir Francis

Bacon! Sir Francis Bacon! Sir Francis Bacon, thou cream-faced loon!"

But he did not.

Instead, he bowed lowly and said, "My apologies, William. I mean, Mr. Shakespeare. Mr. William Shakespeare. Willie. The Bard of Avon. The Great Bard. The Bard of Shadows."

Sir Francis smiled. "That's better, good and faithful companion. Remember, as I always say, "What's in a name? That which we call a rose by any other name would smell as sweet.' So, why doth thou come to disturb me?"

"My apologies, Bill," Cedric replied, feeding into the man's alter ego. "But I am simply following thou's instructions. You said for me to check in on thee if neither I nor or any of the staff layeth eyes upon thee for a prodigious period of time."

"I said that?"

"Verily."

"Verily? Truly?"

"Truly verily."

"And when did I giveth such a command? I do not recalleth."

"Two days ago."

"Two days ago? Fie away, sir. I find that difficult to believe."

"One needs only to take a breath of this room to know that it is the truth, Sir . . ., I mean, William."

Sir Francis took hold of his blouse and held it out while lowering his head to take a sniff. "By my gammer's withered leg!" he exclaimed. "That is the rankest of the rank."

"Thou tellest me! My eyes doth still water like the dew falling from the petals of a morning bloom."

"Hmmm, I like that one. I must remember to write it down sometime," the bard said from his desk.

"What, pray tell, are you currently working on, Master Shakespeare?"

"One of my best works so far, I believe with all my heart of hearts."

Cedric shrugged. "Yes, but you sayeth that about everything you write."

"But this time, it really be the bee's knees."

"Does it have a title yet?"

"*The Taming of the Shrew*," Sir Francis declared triumphantly.

"The Taming of a Shrew? A shrew? One of those tiny, mole-like vermin that runneth around in the fields?" Cedric asked with a perplexed countenance.

"Nay. Nay," Sir Francis said with a broad wave of his hand. "Not the dram animal. I speaketh about the most dangerous of shrew—a bad-tempered, rampallian mistress."

"Ah," nodded the knowing Cedric. "Like your wife, Lady Bacon."

"Yes. Wait. I mean no. Not like dear Alice."

"*Dear* Alice?"

"Very well," Sir Francis begrudgingly conceded. "The course of true love never did run smooth. After all, I am one who loved not wisely but too well."

"Alas, so it is a tragedy?" the servant inquired. A look of confusion on his face.

"Nay. A comedy! A light-hearted, feel-good romp if ever there was one."

"About a shrewish woman," Cedric said, the doubt evident in his voice.

"Aye. You see, she starts out a shrewish woman. Katharina is her name. The play concerneth her volatile courtship with the clever Petruchio, who is determined to subdue his Kate's legendary temper and also receiveth her dowry. Through his cunning, he doth changes her into a loving, compliant mate. Here, let me read to thee what I just wrote,

"This is a way to kill a wife with kindness,
And thus I'll curb her mad and headstrong humour.
He that knows better how to tame a shrew,
Now let him speak. Tis charity to show."

Cedric rubbed his chin and suggested, "It sounds to me as though thou art hoping life wouldst imitate art as in the case of your *dear* Alice."

"Love looks not with the eyes, but with the mind; and therefore is winged Cupid painted blind."

"What does that mean?" inquired Cedric.

"I have no idea," answered Sir Francis. "I just needed some sort of comeback to distract thee from pointing out the foibles of my marriage."

"Very well then, bid me what is this shrewish Kate's age in the play?"

"I doth not sayeth. She could be a virginal thirteen or a matronly thirty-five. Tis up to the audience to interpret such. Personally, I envision her as a younger lass but spirited and untamed."

"Enough with the thirteen-year-old girls, Sir Francis."

"William."

"Whatever," replied the long-suffering servant. "My point is, your female characters are often much too young, even for our time. Tis creepy."

"Creepy? Nay!"

"William, alloweth me to asketh thee this question then. How old was dear Alice when thou married her?"

Sir Francis looked toward the ceiling to do the math in his head before saying, "She was thirteen." But then he quickly added, "But she was nearly fourteen."

"Thirteen it is then. And how old were you when you married her?"

Bacon looked toward the ceiling again to do the math in his head before saying, "Um, forty-five?"

"Correct. *Forty-five*," he emphasized. "And creepy I might addeth."

"Methinks thou doth protest too much," Sir Francis shot back. "After all, Juliet was a winsome young woman of just thirteen and everyone loved my play *Romeo and Juliet*."

Cedric grimaced. "To bid the sooth, I hath heard from the late queen's staff that her majesty, Elizabeth, was uncomfortable with Juliet's age as well."

"Nay!" cried out Sir Francis. "I doth not believeth it. Anyway, her nephew, King James the First reigns upon us now. I am sure he didst not have any problems with her age."

"Well," Cedric said after letting out a long breath. "I have also heard from his staff that King James is . . ." He pauses, looks around and whispers, "A Greek enthusiast."

"A what?"

"A Greek enthusiast," he said a little louder.

"Well, who isn't?" Sir Francis replied with a slap to his knee. "Plato's *Republic*. Homer's *Iliad* and *Odyssey*. Aristotle. Pythagoras. Euripides."

"Euripides you pay for them," they said in unison.

"Always a good one," Sir Francis chuckled. "Who dost not enjoy the great Greek masters?"

"Nay. Nay. A Greek enthusiast," Cedric whispers even louder now, noticing his master's incomprehension. "Thou knoweth . . ."

"Knoweth what?"

"Oh for crying out loud," Cedric said aloud. "In *Romeo and Juliet*, His Majesty would not be looking at Juliet as a fetching young girl but rather . . . "

"Rather what?"

Exasperated, Cedric finally said, "He would much more be likely to be checking Romeo's codpiece than Juliet's bodice, if you knoweth what I mean."

"Impossible! They named an entire Bible after him!"

"Tis true. Upon my mother's grave."

"Ooooooh. Well, he *IS* Scottish, after all," Sir Francis said as he dismissed the subject with his hand.

"Art thou sure this *Taming of the Shrew* would not be better as a tragedy instead?"

"Aye, I considered it. But the comedies selleth better, and I am a dram short of funds anon."

"Now and always," mumbled the long-suffering Cedric. "Have thou ever considered revealing thy true identity rather than using yond merchant from Avon as the author? Perhaps the public wouldst respondeth better. After all, dost not everyone loveth Bacon?"

He raised his hand in refusal. "Nay. Let Sir Francis Bacon be Sir Francis Bacon. Let the world have one of its own as William Shakespeare. As I hath always said, 'All the world's a stage, and all the men and women merely players. They have their exits and their entrances; And one man in his time plays many parts.' This is one of the most wondrous tragedies in the world, that I shall never be known for my genius. But that is how it must be. I must merely play a part."

"Very well . . . William," Cedric responded with a bow. "Along with 'All the world's a stage,' dost thou have any other pithy sayings?"

Sir Francis blew out another giant breath as he thought for a moment. "Very well," he said at last. "Some are born great, some achieve greatness, and some have greatness thrust upon them."

Cedric nodded in agreement.

"Brevity is the soul of wit."

"Well said—and brief," pointed out the servant.

"Um, all that glitters is not gold."

"Although some more gold wouldst be helpful considering thy financial state," Cedric added. "Any more pearls of wisdom?"

"Let's see. How about 'Neither a borrower nor a lender be.' Or, 'Guests, like fish, begin to smell after three days.' Oh here's one I like, "Three men can keep a secret, if two are dead.'"

"Those are very good. Will you be using them in one of your plays?"

He paused for a moment to ponder. "Nay, I think not. I think I shall passeth on these sayings to mine own Freemason brethren at Rosslyn Chapel in Scotland, along with copies of my plays for them to hide and store in the New World, where they can be used by other Freemasons there to elucidate future generations. These are trying times here in England, and a foul wind may soon bloweth me and the works of William Shakespeare out of favor, never to be heardeth in these lands again."

Cedric was about to voice his protestations, but a voice from downstairs shouted up, "Here now! Frank!

I'm planning to wend out with the girls. I need some money!"

"Yes, dear," a dejected Sir Francis, the true Bard of Avon, called back as he got out his coin purse and made his way past his servant to go down to his wife.

As he stood alone in the room, Cedric looked over to the play his master had been working on and said, "*The Taming of the Shrew*. A *fictional comedy* by a fictional William Shakespeare."

4

GEORGE WASHINGTON

A TOAST TO SOMETHING, SOMETHING WASHINGTON

"Mr. Adams! Mr. Adams! Please join me for a moment. It is of the upmost importance."

Sighing, the stern John Adams stopped his purposeful walk down the hallway, turned around, and went into the officious office. "Yes, George," he said as he settled uncomfortably into the unadorned wooden chair before him, well aware that everything seemed to be of the "upmost importance" to the fledgling leader of the new nation.

"You see. You see. That's the problem," George replied while settling into a chair behind his desk. "I've been in office a week now. I should not be called 'George' or 'Mr. Washington' or even "General Washington'—for crying out loud, the War of Independence ended six years ago."

He slapped the Brobdingnagian desk for effect and then adjusted his wig, which had slid forward a couple of inches because of the impact.

"Yes, sir. Whatever you say, sir. Do you have ideas, sir?" his compliant, grumpy vice president asked.

"Hmmm." He sat back in his Brobdingnagian chair, which groaned under his great weight. "I really had not given it much thought."

"You never do," Adams mumbled.

"What was that?"

"Oh, nothing, sir," Adams said before trying to deflect attention from his comment. "What about getting Ben Franklin to come up with a title for you? He is a clever man."

"The man wanted the turkey to be our national bird. A turkey!" Washington replied in disgust. "The eagle is so much more bad ass." He then leaned forward and whispered, "Is that a term that is in usage? 'Bad ass?' Can we say that?"

"You are in charge, sir. It is now in the lexicon of Americana." He paused to think a moment. "Lexicon or vernacular? I always get the two confused."

Washington shrugged.

"Whatever," Washington said. "I don't trust Franklin to come up with a proper title for me. I need something not too flashy, but something that says I am a man of the peasants."

"People."

"People. Right," Washington replied.

"Like when you made up that cockamamie story about cutting down the cherry tree when you were a child and then confessing to your father to show how honest you are?"

"Exactly."

"The people tried to make you king and call you 'King George,' but you were smart enough to nip that in the bud. I'm sure we can come up with something for you." He thought a second. "How about 'President Washington'? After all, you are the president."

"I suppose. I mean, 'President Washington' does sound good. But that's more of a title to the office. I need something for when I go see Congress or walk down the street amongst the peasants."

"People," Adams corrected.

"People. Right." He then expanded, "I'm looking more for a salutation than title."

Adams looked up the ceiling in thought.

"Just spit balling here, sir. Lord Washington?"

"Hmm. No. Still too royal."

"Chief Washington? After all, you are commander-in-chief. Plus, all the Indian Americans would probably like it."

"Yes, but they can't vote anyway."

"Grand Poohbah Washington?"

Washington scowled.

"Big Kahuna Washington?"

"Big Ka-who-what?"

"It's a word from the Sandwich Islands. British Captain James Cooke discovered them in the Pacific Ocean about eleven years ago."

"Huh, learn something every day," Washington replied. "But no. Too obscure"

"It could catch on. Like 'Brobdingnagian,' which I'm sure will remain in popular usage for centuries to come."

"No doubt, but no."

Adams sighed again. "Okay, how about this? Some people already call you the 'Father of our Country.' So how about Father Washington?"

"Egad, no. Martha might get the wrong idea." He then leaned forward and explained, "She already thinks I spent most of the Revolutionary War just flitting about the country having fun with my buddies and dalliances with admiring lady friends. She still thinks we could have won the blasted conflict in half the time if not for that."

Adams threw up his hands. "Well, I'm out of ideas."

Washington grunted, then stood up and walked to the window to think. While looking down from his second-story window, he spotted a familiar figure half-walking, half-dancing down the New York sidewalk. He leaned out and shouted, "Hamilton! Hey, Alexander!"

Hamilton stopped his jig, looked up, smiled upon recognition of who was calling him, and yelled back, "Hello, Mr. President!"

Washington wheeled around to Adams. "'Mr. President.' I kind of like that. Simple. Dignified. Something a peasant could remember."

"Person," Adams interjected.

"Yes, a 'person' could remember."

He turned to the window and looked down to thank his Secretary of the Treasury, but Hamilton had already resumed his dance down the street while singing to himself, "My name is Alexander Hamilton, and there's a million things I haven't done. But just you wait, just you wait . . ."

Washington leaned back in.

"Well, now that is settled," Adams said. "Perhaps we should come up with a spiffy title for me."

Washington looked at him. "What for? You're just the vice president. You don't do a thing."

Adams looked down at the floor and mumbled, "Brobdingnagian twit."

"What was that?"

"Oh, nothing, Mr. President. Nothing."

5

FRANCIS SCOTT KEY

WHOSE BROAD STRIPES AND BRIGHT STAR THOUGH THE PERILOUS WARS

A determined Francis Scott Key and Prisoner Exchange Agent Colonel John Stuart Skinner strode across the deck of the *HMS Tonnant* and into Vice Admiral Alexander Cochrane's quarters, followed closely by a pair of armed British Royal Marines.

"Admiral Cochrane, I should have expected to find you holding General Ross's leash. I recognized your foul stench when I was brought onboard the *Tonnant*."

"Ah, Francis Scott Key. Charming to the last. You don't know how hard I found it, signing the order to terminate your life."

“I’m surprised you had the courage to take the responsibility yourself.”

“Mr. Key, before your execution, you will join me at a ceremony that will make this battle force operational. No American forts or city defenses will dare oppose the British Empire now.”

“The more the British Empire tightens its grip, Cochrane, the more countries will slip through your fingers.”

“Not after we demonstrate the power of this British naval fleet. In a way, you have determined the choice of the fort and city that is to be destroyed. Since you are reluctant to provide us with the location of the American forces, I have chosen to test our armada’s destructive power on Fort McHenry and the city of Baltimore.”

“No! Fort McHenry is peaceful. They have no weapons. Those aren’t cannons. They are flowerpots that just look like cannons. And Baltimore is filled with no one but widows and orphans who spend all their time doing needlepoint and crocheting and nerfherding.”

“You would prefer another target? Then tell me where the American troops and ships are.” He stepped closer to the American. “I grow tired of asking this, so it will be the last time. Where are the American forces?”

“Washington City. They are regrouping at Washington City.”

“There, you see General Ross? He can be reasonable. Proceed with his execution and then you can fire when ready.”

“What?” the incredulous American lawyer screamed.

"You are far too trusting, Mr. Key. We already burned your capital, Washington, down three weeks ago, and it is too remote to make an effective demonstration. But don't worry. We will deal with your rebellious friends soon enough."

He nodded at the guards to take Key and Skinner out for their execution, but British Major General Robert Ross leaned in and whispered into his ear.

"Really?" responded Cochrane. "They are truce agents? So, I'm not allowed to execute them?"

He looked the Americans over with disgust and said, "Well, that stinks. I'm told I have to release you along with some American doctor we have locked up named William Beanes."

"So sorry to disappoint you," Key answered defiantly.

Wait!" Colonel Skinner called out. "So we are free to go our own way?"

"I'm sorry, but I cannot allow that at this time," Vice Admiral Cochrane replied.

"And why is that?" Skinner demanded.

Because you know too much of our plans," the British commander informed them. "You know our strength and where we plan to strike. After we have destroyed your fort, I shall let you return the prisoner to your precious President Madison."

"The fort will be with you, always." Francis Scott Key retorted.

"You do know your cause is lost. Nothing can withstand the firepower of this fully armed and operational battle fleet."

"We must keep our faith in the Republic. The day we stop believing democracy can work is the day we lose it," Key stated fervently.

"Noble words, indeed." He then motioned to the marines. "Guards, transfer them to our British warship, the *HMS Surprize*, and then to their own sloop to watch their fort be utterly obliterated."

After being moved to their sloop, which was tethered to a British troopship about eight miles from Fort McHenry, Francis Scott Key asked one of his guards, "May we move to the starboard side of the ship so that we may watch the battle?"

"Starboard?" one marine whispered to the other.

"That's the right," the other pointed out.

"All right, this way, you rebel scum," the first marine said as he prodded them with his musket to the ship's railing.

"Very well," Key said as he and his companions were forced by bayonet to the starboard side of the ship. "But technically, we won our war of independence around thirty years ago, so we are no longer rebel scum. However, you are still an evil empire. An important distinction."

"Just do as you are told," said the marine just as he hit his head on a low-hanging piece of the ship's rigging. "Owww!"

"Wait, Francis," Colonel Skinner said, placing his hand on his friend's arm and then nodding toward his head. "Why are you wearing those enormous brown earmuffs?"

"I'm cold."

"Yes, but it's September," Skinner reminded him. "Very well, then. I would suggest you never wear them again after this. They look ridiculous."

In front of them, the sound of the gun ports opening on fifty ships could be heard.

"Do you know what's going on?" the first marine asked.

"Maybe it's just another drill," his fellow marine answered.

Suddenly a giant roar let loose from the *HMS Surprize's* thirty-eight guns and the HMS Torrant's eighty guns, and their ship's small deck shook violently from the reverberation as the cannon and rockets made their way in the direction of Fort McHenry. Almost simultaneously, all the other ships in the British fleet also fired in the fort's direction.

Everything missed to the left.

"Egad," said Colonel Skinner. "These troopers can't hit the side of a barn."

Soon the smoke enveloped them and they could no longer see the fort, the sky, or the ships beside them. "It's like a storm out there with all this smoke," Dr. Beanes yelled out over the din of battle. "Bloody British!"

"Hey!" one of the marines said, his feeling obviously hurt.

"Oh, very well. Present company excepted," Beans replied.

"That's better," the marine said with a snort. He then muttered, "Rebel scum."

"Poor blighters," moaned Colonel Skinner. "They haven't got a chance. Fifty ships all trained on one fort. Eventually they will hit something. The odds are against them."

"Never tell me the odds!" shouted Key as another barrage was directed to the island where the fort stood, the smoke hiding it completely from view.

During the course of the night they listened to the cannon fire and watched as far as they could the red glare of the rockets before the arcs disappeared into the smoke.

Key looked up at the night sky. "Bombs bursting in air," he mumbled to himself because none of the others would have been able to hear him over the noise.

Still, the three men paced and watched, seeing if they could spot anything. "By Jove, this is exhilarating," Key cried out at one point. He turned to the marines and shouted, "I'll be right back." And he rushed past them to his cabin. The marines looked at Skinner and Beanes and shrugged; the Americans shrugged back.

Upon his return, Key held in his hands a pen and paper. "Gentlemen, I am inspired! I must write this down."

"You are inspired and must write down the destruction of our fort?" Skinner asked.

"I find your lack of faith disturbing," Key answered. "No. The battle. I must put prose to paper describing my feelings at this perilous time. I must do this, but it is so difficult under these conditions. Still, I can try, I suppose."

"Do. Or do not. There is no try," Dr. Beanes admonished him.

Key nodded and stood by a keg and wrote, "When Johnny comes marching home again, hurrah."

"No. That's not quite right." And he scratched it out before writing, "Over there. Over there. Send the word, send the word. Over there."

"Close, but that's not it either." And again, he scratched it out. This time he wrote, "I'm Dreaming of a White Christmas."

"Whoa, where did that come from? That one is not even close." And he scratched it out as well. Key then looked in the direction of the fort for inspiration. Dawn was breaking, and by its early light he and his companions were astounded to see the enormous American flag still waving, which meant the fort had not fallen but had withstood the bombardment.

"I cannot believe it," Colonel Skinner declared. "It still stands! They truly cannot hit the side of a womp rat!"

"That's it! I can do this now," Francis Scott Key announced. And he began furiously writing as his companion stood by and watched the British ships begin to withdraw. Within minutes he had finished and showed them his work:

O say can you see, by the dawn's early light,
What so proudly we hailed at the twilight's last gleaming,
Whose broad stripes and bright stars through the perilous fight,
O'er the ramparts we watched, were so gallantly streaming?
And the rocket's red glare, the bombs bursting in air,
Gave proof through the night that our flag was still there;
O say does that star-spangled banner yet wave
O'er the land of the free and the home of the brave?

On the shore dimly seen through the mists of the deep,
Where the foe's haughty host in dread silence reposes,
What is that which the breeze, o'er the towering steep,
As it fitfully blows, half conceals, half discloses?
Now it catches the gleam of the morning's first beam,
In full glory reflected now shines in the stream:
'Tis the star-spangled banner, O long may it wave
O'er the land of the free and the home of the brave.

And where is that band who so vauntingly swore
That the havoc of war and the battle's confusion,
A home and a country, should leave us no more?
Their blood has washed out their foul footsteps' pollution.
No refuge could save the hireling and slave
From the terror of flight, or the gloom of the grave:
And the star-spangled banner in triumph doth wave,
O'er the land of the free and the home of the brave.

O thus be it ever, when freemen shall stand
Between their loved homes and the war's desolation.
Blest with vict'ry and peace, may the Heav'n rescued land
Praise the Power that hath made and preserved us a nation!
Then conquer we must, when our cause it is just,
And this be our motto: 'In God is our trust.'
And the star-spangled banner in triumph shall wave
O'er the land of the free and the home of the brave!

-

"What do you think?" Key asked his companions.

"It's a good poem," Skinner answered.

"It's not a poem," Key corrected him. "These are song lyrics."

"Song lyrics? But you are known as an amateur poet."

"Yes, but I had a song stuck in my head that I could not get rid of and putting these words to the music seemed to work out well."

"What song are these lyrics for, then?" asked Skinner.

"John Stafford Smith's 'To Anacreon in Heaven,'" replied the author.

"'To Anacreon in Heaven'?" an incredulous Skinner said. "But that is one of the most difficult tunes in the world to sing. The range is maddening. No one gets it right."

"That may be, but it works with my lyrics."

"Very well, then. So, what are you calling this song?" Skinner inquired.

"Defence of Fort M'Henry," the proud American lawyer answered.

"McHenry, you mean." Skinner stated.

"That's what I said, 'Fort M'Henry.'"

"Whatever," replied Colonel Skinner. "I suppose the people will choose a better title if they feel the need. Perhaps something like 'The Star Wars Spangled Banner.'"

"What does 'spangled' mean?" inquired Key.

"Who knows," the colonel responded. "Spangled banner is just very catchy."

A slightly flustered Dr. Beanes spoke up. "Isn't anyone concerned about the racist phrase in the third stanza?"

"Don't worry about it," said Key. "It's 1814. It's the South. Slavery is still going strong. Even if it does end someday, people probably won't be bothered by the lyrics for another couple hundred years, and we will all be dead and gone. Plus, be honest, does anyone ever read the third stanzas of these patriotic anthems anyway?"

As he finished with his statement, their two marine guards walked past them to leave the American boat and retire with the rest of their fleet. As he was about to go over the side, the last marine turned to the Americans and said, "You can have your fort and your ridiculous 'anthem' or whatever it is. But remember, the British Empire will strike back."

6

NAPOLÉON BONAPARTE

METRICS FOR SUCCESS

The dashing, young cavalryman rode erect and confidently into the French camp, dismounting and saluting the nearest ranking officer he could find.

"Mon capitaine," he said breathlessly, "I am Lieutenant Babineaux. I have an urgent message from Maréchal Ney for the emperor."

The French captain looked the tall young officer up, then down, and shook his head. "Mon dieu. What is Ney thinking?"

"Monsieur?"

How tall are you, Lieutenant?"

"Um, six feet three inches," he replied before adding, "I apologize. I do not know what that is in the emperor's new metric system as that has yet to have taken hold."

"Why does Maréchal Ney despise you?"

"Monsieur?"

The grizzled captain shook his head and looked at the younger man.

"Have you done something to make Ney angry with you?"

The confused-looking young officer said, "Not that I am aware, Capitaine. I am a brave and exemplary officer." He then paused and added, "Unless . . ."

"Unless?"

"Well," the young officer replied sheepishly. "There was the matter of me recently dating his young cousin in Paris." He again paused before revealing, "It did not end well, I am afraid."

"Oui, young Babineaux. You should be afraid."

"May ask why, monsieur?"

"The emperor is très competitive. Hence, why he wants to take over all of Europe."

"But what does that have to do with me, Capitaine?"

"Général Bonaparte is extremely sensitive about his height. He has seen the reports from all over Europe about how short he is, and it displeases him greatly."

"But I have seen him from a distance. He is of average height for a man of our day. I mean, I am sure someday, when we all can eat healthier foods and modern medicine has eradicated disease and we have machines we may hang upside down on, people—on average—will be taller. But he is of normal height."

"Oui. That is the problem. That word you used. 'Average.' He cannot be 'average.' He is Napoléon Bonaparte. Jupiter Scapin. Emperor of the French. He cannot be average."

"But that is ridiculous! He conquered Europe. He is the greatest military leader in French history. Surely he cannot be bothered because I am a little taller?"

"Oui. He most certainly can and will be bothered. The only reason I have survived so long is because I am five centimeters shorter than is he."

"Then what am I to do, Capitaine? I have been ordered to personally give him a message."

The grizzled capitaine circled the young lieutenant before saying, "Slouch."

"What?"

"Slouch as though your life depends on it—which it may."

"You cannot be serious."

"Very well. Stand up as straight as you can and see how he reacts."

The young officer pondered his two options for a moment before slouching his entire body as much as he could and hanging his head in front of him, knowing he looked as ridiculous as he felt.

“It is what it is,” the capitaine said with a shrug. “I will take you into the command tent to see him, so you can deliver your message.”

Babineaux nodded and proceeded to follow his superior officer toward the tent. Suddenly, the older man stopped and wheeled around. “Oh, and I should warn you. Because of the height anxieties, the emperor often stuffs newspapers in his boot because he thinks it makes him a little taller. It does not, in fact. The only thing it does is make him sway back and forth from time to time as he struggles to maintain his balance. Do NOT say anything or act like you notice.”

The officer nodded in understanding and began walking in step behind the capitaine, who once again turned abruptly before saying, “Oh, and speaking of things to act like you do not notice, do not pay attention to his habit of putting his hand inside his waistcoat.”

“His hand inside his waistcoat?”

“Oui. He happens to have a third nipple there and he likes touching it, thinking it brings him bon chance. You know, one of the typical megalomaniac quirks that many emperors and générals have.” He added, “I have heard that even Prussian general, von Blücher—“ A horse whinnied loudly nearby, causing both men to look. “He keeps a pet duck in his tent because he believes it wards off demons.”

As they neared the opening of the tent, the now-fearful officer stopped and said, “Wait. What should I call him? Is he still Emperor Bonaparte since he has returned from exile or Général Bonaparte because he commands our troops in the field?"

The older officer shrugged and said, "That is what today's battle shall decide." He then nodded for the young man to follow him in.

"My emperor," the capitaine announced upon entering the tent. "Lieutenant Babineaux is here with a message for you from Maréchal Ney."

Général Napoléon Bonaparte turned from the map on the table before him and strode to the young officer who simultaneously attempted to stand at attention, slouch, and salute while staring straight ahead to avoid looking down at his commanding officer and making the height differential even more obvious.

He stared above the young officer's head down to his feet while swaying from heel to toe. "One hundred ninety."

The confused young man said, "I'm sorry, mon général. What?"

"One hundred ninety centimeters."

Lieutenant Babineaux gave a sideways glance to the capitaine, who was discreetly nodding back to him.

"Um. Yes, sir. I believe so."

"I knew it! If there is one thing of which I am sure, it is the metric system. That is why we are fighting this war, Lieutenant. I do not care about power. It is the English arrogance I despise. Were you aware that they claim credit for inventing the metric system? What a load of merde! The French invented the metric system decades ago, and I, Napoléon Bonaparte, am the one making sure it is implemented in every land we conquer."

Babineaux did his best to slouch even more during the rant, not wanting his height to be the subject of his leader's next tirade. But he could tell his commander was displeased with him.

"Oh, very well, Lieutenant Girafe, what is the message from my général from the Army of the North?"

The young soldier took note of the received insult of being called that long-necked animal from Africa but knew better than to reply in kind. Although he was tempted to mention his emperor's unsteady gait due to the newspapers stuffed in his boots.

"Maréchal Ney said to inform you that the left wing is prepared to attack Wellington's forces. He has ordered a mass calvary charge against the Anglo-Allied lines and intends to overrun the enemy's cannons."

"Bon!" Napoléon shouted before striding over to the giant map to look it over again. "I shall attack von Blücher—" A nearby horse whinnied loudly, causing all the officers to look toward the tent opening. "And we shall move a few kilometers on the Prussians' rear to cut off their line of retreat. And then we shall drink a litre of champagne to celebrate." He then whispered to the capitaine. "Is a litre enough? I myself forget sometimes how much that is."

The capitaine shrugged.

Napoléon paced around the tent as though deep in thought. Lieutenant Babineaux, growing excited about the upcoming battle and its foregone outcome took it upon himself to ask, “My emperor, if I may. Once we have conquered Europe and England, what are your plans then?

The Corsican général stopped pacing and looked up at the young man. With a confident smile, he said, “Then I shall go and offer to teach the Americans our metric system. I am sure they will appreciate it. After all, I sold them the Louisiana Purchase for a song. They will see our new scientific way of measuring's value and switch over to it immediately. American's love new things.” He then looked back down at his map. “Waterloo,” he sneered. “It sounds like an English toilet. Today Waterloo belongs to Wellington and . . .” He looked around and whispered, “von Blücher.” A nearby horse whinnied loudly. “But after I thrash them both to within a centimeter of their lives, it will not be Wellington's Waterloo, but it will forever be known as Napoléon's Waterloo.”

7

ABRAHAM LINCOLN

87 YEARS AGO--THE GETTYSBURG ADDRESS

The plodding train lurched suddenly, causing the contently napping president to jerk his head up and look around to find his bearings.

"Back amongst the living, Mr. President?" William Seward, Abraham Lincoln's secretary of state, asked from across the aisle.

"It would appear so, Mr. Seward. It would appear so."

The president then stretched out his long legs as best he could, mindful not to kick his personal secretary, John Nicolay, as he did so. "Out of curiosity, Mr. Nicolay, how were you able to keep Mrs. Lincoln from wanting to come along on this trip to Gettysburg?"

Nicolay squirmed uncomfortably in his seat and then stammered, "Uh, well, to tell the truth, Mr. President, I told her right before we left that I thought I had seen the ghost of her maternal grandmother wandering aimlessly in the root cellar. And she skedaddled that direction as fast as she could to talk to her."

Lincoln nodded and smiled slightly. "Thank you, Mr. Nicolay."

Seward leaned forward and said, "Thank you, Mr. Nicolay."

"Well, that would seem to free up a copious amount of my schedule. I shall now have time to write my address."

"Your address, Mr. President?" Seward asked incredulously. "You mean we're nearly there, and you haven't written it yet?"

"No. I kept meaning to, but something was always coming up. You know. War stuff. Sherman accidently burning down Atlanta and then trying to blame it all on the Confederates leaving town. Then Grant getting drunk and riding his horse into that house of ill repute in Arlington and tearing the place apart." He shook his head. "That took months of negotiations and bribes to keep those dear fallen angels all quiet."

"Yes," Seward acknowledged. "We notice how often you would journey there to, um, 'negotiate.'"

"Nevertheless, Mr. Nicolay, bring me a writing desk and some paper."

"Your writing desk? Your portable writing desk?" John Nicolay asked nervously.

"Yes. Is there a problem?"

A clearly uncomfortable Nicolay cleared his throat. "Uh, I don't seem to have it, Mr. President. I mean, I did have it. But now I don't."

"And when was the last time you remember having it?"

"I definitely brought it with me from the White House to the train station. It was in my arms. I remember that."

"And then, Mr. Nicolay?"

"I then decided to use the privy by the train station before the trip. I set it down outside. I went inside and relieved myself, which was greater than I expected. Probably because I had turnips last night for dinner. And then I came out. Got on the train. And . . ."

"And so you are saying my writing desk is sitting outside an outhouse in Washington?"

"Actually, Mr. President," Seward interjected. "I'm sure it has probably been stolen by now."

"Thank you, Mr. Seward," the president replied. "Not helpful. But thank you."

"As soon as we pull into the station, I can telegraph Mr. Hay back at the capitol and have him go down and look for it," Nicolay offered as helpfully as he could.

"I suppose," Lincoln sighed. "Very well, get me some paper and I'll push this speech out as quickly as those turnips left poor Mr. Nicolay."

Nicolay's eyes opened wide. "Paper?"

"It was in the desk, wasn't it, John," Lincoln said as he got out his reading glasses and put them on.

"Yes, Mr. President. Sorry, sir."

With that, Lincoln pulled an envelope from his pocket. "I guess this will have to do. I shall write it down on this. The added benefit is that it will force me to keep it short and sweet."

"Yes, that and the fact that we are almost there," Seward added.

"You're a regular Greek chorus today, aren't you William."

Seward shrugged.

Lincoln looked down at the back of the envelope. Just as he was about to write, the train hit a bump, sending the three of them into the air.

"Hang on, boys," he said. "It's going to be a bumpy ride. But we'll figure out a way to gitter done."

He looked down again and furrowed his brow before smiling and saying aloud, "Eight-seven years ago, ol' George Washington and his cronies decided to stick it to ol' King George."

Seward looked like he had just been struck by a Confederate musket ball. "Really? 'Eighty-seven years ago, ol' George Washington and his cronies decided to stick it to ol' King George?'"

"Yes. What's wrong with that?"

"This is a solemn, officious occasion, Mr. President. It is not politicking with the yokels by the whiskey barrel in New Salem, Illinois."

"I suppose," Lincoln relented. "So does that mean I can't include the joke about a priest, a rabbi and Jefferson David walking into a tavern?"

"And you especially cannot tell that one. There will be ladies present. Not your 'dear fallen angels.'"

"Very well, Mr. Seward. But it does always get a laugh."

"Yes, it does, Mr. President. But this is solemn and officious."

Lincoln looked to the roof of the train car and pondered. "Solemn and officious, eh?"

His two traveling companions nodded fervently, hoping the tall, gangly rural-born president would comprehend the gravitas of the next day's ceremony.

"How about "Eight-seven years ago, our fathers brought forth, on this continent, a new nation, conceived in liberty, and dedicated to the proposition that all men and women are created equal."

"Women?" A suspicious Seward asked.

"Ah, I'm just yankin' your chain," Lincoln laughed and said. "All MEN are created equal."

Seward chuckled as much as he was capable of any kind of mirth—which was not much.

"Mr. President, if I may suggest," interrupted John Nicolay. "Starting a solemn speech with a number. It just doesn't sound . . ."

"Professional," Seward finished.

"Very well."

"And are you sure it was eighty-seven years ago?" Nicolay asked.

All three of them looked up toward the ceiling of the train car. Lincoln mumbled, "Let's see. 1864. 1777." And he began calculating the math in his head while Seward had his hand out and was counting on his fingers.

"Yes, eighty-seven," they both said together.

"I'm glad that's settled," the president announced. "But what instead?"

Nicolay perked up and said, "How about, 'A long time ago in a galaxy far, far away'?"

Lincoln looked at him as if he had seen one of Mary's apparitions. "What are you talking about?"

"Oh, nothing. It's just something my cousin Hiram George Lucas always says." He added, "He's been a little touched in the brain ever since his mule, Luke, kicked him in the head at his ranch in California. He's always saying you're an evil emperor. And you're trying to force stuff on the people. Or something like that."

"Mmmm. I don't know how to respond to that, so let's just ignore it and move on."

"Score," Seward said suddenly.

"Excuse me?" Lincoln asked.

"Score. It means twenty," Seward explained. "It comes from the Old Norse word, *skor*."

"I am learning far more than I had hoped to today," Abraham Lincoln said. "So how does this help me?"

"We divide eighty-seven by it."

"I may not have gone to school, Mr. Seward, but I do know that eighty-seven does not divide evenly by score."

"No, Mr. President. You divide the number by how many scores are in it and then the remainder."

"So eighty-seven would be . . ." his voice trailed off as all three of them had their hands out and started doing the division in their heads.

"Fourscore and seven?" Nicolay timidly offered.

Lincoln and Seward looked at each other and shrugged.

"Sounds good to me," the sixteenth president said. "But will anyone in the crowd understand it?"

"That's the beauty of it, Mr. President," Nicolay explained. "Probably not. So, you will sound like their intellectual superior and dazzle them with your knowledge."

"Hmm, I like that."

He lowered his head, his beard resting upon his chest, and continued to write feverishly right up until the train began slowing down as it arrived at the station.

"Finished. And just in time," he said as he peered out the window to the crowd of people awaiting him on the railroad platform. "A masterpiece, if I do say so myself. Certainly an opus worthy of the keynote speaker."

"Keynote speaker?" Nicolay interjected. "I'm sorry, Mr. President, but you are not the keynote speaker. You shall be following his speech with yours."

Lincoln's eyebrows flared. "What? But I am the president of the United States! I am the commander in chief! Who in blazes did they get to hog all my glory?"

It was Seward's turn to answer. "Edward Everett, Mr. President. The greatest orator in the land."

"Greatest orator," a perturbed Lincoln countered. "If you equate greatness to the amount of time the man stands up there and will not shut his pie hole, then yes, he is the greatest orator in the world."

Seward sought to sooth the hurt feelings. "Now Abraham. It is what it is. This is a time to accept what we cannot change and for you to be the bigger man."

"I am six feet four inches tall, William. I am always the bigger man."

"Of course, sir."

As they attended the ceremony the next day, Lincoln looked respectfully from his chair while Edward Everett talked . . . and talked . . . and talked . . . and talked . . . and then talked some more. All the while thinking to himself, "Doesn't this man ever shut up? I had three cups of coffee during breakfast! It would be rude of me to get up and head over to the comfort station tent to relieve myself now. But if he does not stop his never-ending oration soon, that will be what will happen."

Finally, after speaking for a full two hours, Everett ended his speech:

"But they, I am sure, will join us in saying, as we bid farewell to the dust of these martyr-heroes, that wheresoever throughout the civilized world the accounts of this great warfare are read, and down to the latest period of recorded time, in the glorious annals of our common country, there will be no brighter page than that which relates the Battles of Gettysburg."

"Finally," Lincoln thought to himself as he shook the man's hand and pulled out his envelope with his dedicatory speech, waiting for his turn after the Baltimore Glee Club finished its song.

He stood and looked out to the throng of citizens and Union soldiers awaiting his remarks and was glad it was the length it was considering the amount of coffee making its way down his lengthy intestines.

"Four score and seven years ago our fathers brought forth upon this continent, a new nation, conceived in Liberty, and dedicated to the proposition that all men are created equal."

The Great Emancipator looked out to see some people counting on their fingers as they attempted to figure out "fourscore and seven."

'Now we are engaged in a great civil war, testing whether that nation, or any nation so conceived and so dedicated, can long endure. We are met on a great battle-field of that war. We have come to dedicate a portion of that field, as a final resting place for those who here gave their lives that that nation might live. It is altogether fitting and proper that we should do this.

"But, in a larger sense, we can not dedicate—we can not consecrate—we can not hallow—this ground. The brave men, living and dead, who struggled here, have consecrated it, far above our poor power to add or detract. The world will little note, nor long remember what we say here, but it can never forget what they did here. It is for us the living, rather, to be dedicated here to the unfinished

work which they who fought here have thus far so nobly advanced. It is rather for us to be here dedicated to the great task remaining before us—that from these honored dead we take increased devotion to that cause for which they gave the last full measure of devotion—that we here highly resolve that these dead shall not have died in vain—that this nation, under God, shall have a new birth of freedom—and that government of the people, by the people, for the people, shall not perish from the earth."

He then sat down to a smattering of applause as most had not realized he had finished—especially considering the length of Everett's address.

Everett's head jerked up as he suddenly realized Lincoln was finished. "Wait. What?" he thought to himself. "That's it? It was not even two minutes. I spent months working on my address. That sounded like something he just whipped up on the train ride up here. Surely, he would not have done that. What am I to tell the man that will not make me sound petty? I gave an actual address. He came up with a couple of remarks. Come up with something. Come up with something, Edward, old boy."

The next day Edward Everett would sit down and write the president a note saying, "I should be glad, if I could flatter myself that I came as near to the central idea of the occasion, in two hours, as you did in two minutes."

As he posted his passive aggressive letter that pointed the disparity in the lengths of the speeches, Edward said to himself, "Gettysburg Address my sweet patootie.

I gave an address. He just gave some remarks. At least I have the satisfaction of knowing my speech shall go down in the annals or oratory history. Let's see whatever becomes of his!"

8

GEORGE ARMSTRONG CUSTER

THE BATTLE OF GREASY GRASS

The cavalry officer looked out upon the seemingly endless plain of grass before him. The June morning sun was warm, deterring him from putting on his buckskin jacket. Turning, he spotted his well-known older brother in his buckskin jacket having his morning cup of coffee by the campfire.

"George, you are going to be as hot as blazes if you fight while wearing that," he said while pointing to the fringed jacket.

"Captain Custer," his commanding officer replied. "Mother has warned you about not referring to my rank when you address me."

"Oh, for crying out loud, George," his brother, Thomas, replied. "Very well. *Colonel* Custer, you are going to be hot as blazes if you fight in that dang hot coat."

"That's better. Although I do still miss the days when I was General Custer."

"That was eleven years ago during the Civil War, Geor—I mean, Colonel. You were simply brevetted up to general for the war. You cannot expect the Army to let everyone who made general be allowed to keep that rank. We would have had hundreds of 'em running around. And that's the last thing an army needs is more generals than enlisted men."

"Yes, still, some of us earned the rank and deserved to keep it. There is no finer officer in the U.S. Cavalry than George Armstrong Custer. With my military genius and fighting skills, I obviously should still be a general. I am a modern-day Alexander the Great."

"Obviously, brother."

Just then, a grizzled sergeant rode up, quickly dismounted, and smartly saluted the colonel, who returned his salute just as crisply.

"Colonel Custer, sir. I got three injuns just beyond that knoll down yonder carrying a white flag and saying they want to parley. They say it's important."

The elder Custer brightened and said, "That's a surprise. Very brave of those braves." He then chuckled at his own joke. He looked at his younger brother, "Perhaps they wish to surrender and go back to the reservations like we asked."

"Well, technically we never asked. We just told them," Thomas mumbled to himself.

"Sergeant Carlin, bring up one of the Crow scouts to interpret. You shall lead Captain Custer and myself to them to see what they want to parley about."

"Yes, sir," the sergeant replied. "But we ain't gonna be needing no Crow scout to interpret for us. Their leader speaks English better than I do."

"Really? Well, I look forward to hearing that." And with that, he put on his hat with a flourish, and he and his brother mounted their horses and followed the soldier to their rivals a couple hundred yards away.

Upon arriving, the Custer brothers found three warriors in front of them. Two were still astride their ponies with one holding the reins of the third pony. Its disembarked rider was obviously the spokesperson and stood out in front of his companions waiting patiently.

Custer and his brother quickly dismounted, both interested to hear what the man had to say. The leader strode forward to them, stopping to face them eye to eye.

"I am Colonel George Armstrong Custer, 7th Calvary. And this is my brother, Captain Thomas Custer."

The man surprised them by sticking out his hand and shaking their hands in the usual greeting of the white man. He surprised them even more when he said in perfect English, "Gentleman. A pleasure to meet both of you. I certainly hope that we can make good use of this time to settle our grievous disputes. An honest dialect is often helpful when it comes to diffusing quarrels."

The two Custers looked at each other in bewilderment.

"Oh, where are my manners. Let me introduce my colleagues. My comrade on the left with the white flag is Colonel Wooden Leg of the Cheyenne 1st Regiment. And the handsome chap on the right is Colonel Fat Lip of the Arapaho 2nd Regiment." Both native colonels nodded their heads once, knowing they had been introduced. He then turned around and said with a small bow, "And I am Colonel Rain-in-the-Face of the Lakota 1st Regiment."

"Colonel?" Captain Custer inquired.

"Yes. General Crazy Horse decided a couple of years ago that we can no longer just throw groups of warriors together without some organization. So we developed a hierarchy based on your military structure to better organize, train, and conduct ourselves in battle."

"General Crazy Horse?" Captain Custer repeated. "That's going to take some getting used to."

"Not to mention he outranks you now," Thomas chuckled quietly to himself.

"Colonel Rain-in-the-Face, may I say, your English skills are impeccable. How did you acquire them?" Custer asked as he looked over the man standing before him.

"Why, thank you, Colonel Custer," he replied. "I was taught for several years at missionary schools. Most of my people hated them, but I took to them quite well and learned all that I could so I could someday use it against our enemies." And then he beamed a disingenuous smile at them.

The more they spoke, the more George Armstrong Custer seemed to grow even more confused. "That's, um, impressive. So what is the meaning of this meeting today?

"I just wanted a chance to converse with you to try and dissuade you from making an illegal attack upon an aggrieved people."

"Illegal attack? Aggrieved people? How so?"

"The Second Treaty of Fort Laramie, 1868. It says your government cannot push our people off the reservations you designated for the Oceti Sakowin people. The treaty only allowed the United States to build its railroad along the Platt, but it set apart a territory for the Lakota's absolute and undisturbed use and occupation--even if some white men do happen to find gold on them."

"So you're saying you would like for me to gather up my soldiers and just skedaddle from here?"

"Ideally, yes."

Colonel Custer shook his head. "I'm sorry, but your grievances are with the U.S. government. I am just a soldier following orders. If it were up to me, maybe. But I am expected to slaughter every last one of you heathens." He paused. "No offense."

"That's a pity. However, you do understand that you are greatly outnumbered and do not stand a chance."

"Do not stand a chance?" Custer strongly replied. "This is a regiment of the United States Army. The greatest fighting force in the world. Commanded by me, the greatest Indian fighter in the world."

"Well, according to our Intelligence Scouts, we have you outnumbered four, maybe five to one."

"Intelligence Scouts?"

"Yes. And they also note that you have not brought any of your weapons of mass destruction."

"Weapons of what?" a confused Colonel Custer asked.

"Weapons of mass destruction. You know. Your artillery pieces. Your Gatling guns."

It was at that point that Captain Thomas Custer looked at Rain-in-the Face's two companions and noticed one was carrying a Winchester repeating rifle and the other a Spencer repeating rifle, both of which were far superior to his troops' single-shot, breach-loading Springfield carbines. He tugged on his brother's arm. "Uh, George. Maybe we should discuss this."

The older brother jerked his arm away and said, "Discuss nothing. We have our orders."

"I am sorry if that is how you feel, Colonel Custer. I shall report your answer to General Crazy Horse and General Sitting Bull." He gave a slight bow. "My troops and I look forward to facing you in combat today."

"As do we, Colonel Rain-in-the-Face. I am sure the Battle of the Little Bighorn shall go down in the annals of history as one of the greatest our two peoples shall fight between us. And one of the greatest in the chronicles of the United States Army."

"The Battle of what?" Rain-in-the-Face asked.

"Little Bighorn. That's what we call this area."

"Ohhhhhh," the rival native colonel said. "We're calling this the Battle of Greasy Grass."

"Greasy Grass?"

"Yes. It does not translate terribly well, but that is what we call this area."

"Very well, but before you go, I am curious. Do your people still call me 'Yellow Hair'?" the vain glorious man asked while lifting his hat to run his fingers through his sweaty locks.

"We have a great many names for you, Colonel Custer, most of which I am too polite to repeat." And with that, he climbed back on his war pony, and he and his companions rode off to their encampment to prepare for the inevitable fight.

"Battle of Greasy Grass. More like the Battle of Bloody Grass, if you ask me," said Captain Custer after they left.

"That's the spirit, Tom! It will be a massacre!"

"No, George I mean . . . " his brother tried to tell him. "Oh, never mind."

9

ORVILLE AND WILBUR WRIGHT

OUR PLANE/AIRPLANE

“I want to go first.”

“No, I’m the older brother. I should go first,” Wilbur Wright responded to his younger sibling.

“What in the world does that have to do with anything?” Orville asked.

Wilbur raised his head from the pulley system he was tightening on the craft and said, “Because, should this go horribly wrong, it is my duty as the eldest to suffer the brunt of the injuries or even death. That is the way Father would want it, I am sure."

"I think you just want to go and hog all the glory, Will."

Orville looked up and down the ground and over by the sandy dunes at the handful of observers who had come out to help them and who probably were hoping the foolish brothers would fail in a spectacular crash that they could talk about for weeks because there was little else to do in this remote area of the Outer Banks of North Carolina.

"Very well. I don't want to make a scene in front of those people," Wilbur said. "Would it be acceptable to you if we flipped a coin and then took turns afterwards?"

"It would," Orville answered.

Wilbur pulled a coin from his pocket and was about to flip it into the air, when Orville grabbed his older brother's wrist and said, "Wait a minute. I want to check to make sure this isn't one of those doubled-headed coins or whatnot."

He looked at both sides of the silver dollar and noted the woman's head on one side and the eagle on other. Satisfied with what he saw, he looked at his brother and said, "Tails."

Flipping the coin high into the air, Wilbur had to adjust because of the brisk wind to catch it and then flip it onto his wrist. "Tails it is."

Orville grinned broadly and said, "History!"

"Excuse me?"

"History," Orville repeated excitedly. "If successful, we're making history."

The dour Wilbur looked at his brother and said, "Well, I suppose so."

"'Suppose so.' What are you talking about? I will be the first man to ever leave the earth in a powered, heavier-than-air craft. We shall become world famous. Poems shall be written about our bravery. Songs shall be sung about our daring. Dime novels will tell of our exploits here today—except they will probably add some fictionalized details such as a beautiful woman standing bravely by, but also in terror about whether or not I shall survive."

"A beautiful woman?"

"Or they might have bandits riding over the dune at us with six-guns a blazing, and we're forced to flee by flying away just in the nick of time. Surprising them because they have never seen such a sight before."

"How about we just make a successful flight first, Orv? We'll let history sort itself out later on."

"If you say so, Will. But there are still many details we have to work out first."

"Details?" his brother asked as he tightened a cable over the lower wing. "What details? We've been working on our heavier-than-air powered craft for years."

"And you just made my point."

"What point?" Wilbur asked.

"A heavier-than-air powered craft or motorized craft. That's too much of a mouthful. We need something shorter that not only we can use but will catch on with the public," Orville answered.

Wilbur threw up his hands. "Does this really need to be answered right now?"

"Why not right now? This is as good a time as any."

"Well, for one thing, we haven't gotten the, the *thing*, even off the ground yet. And for another, it's the middle of December, and those gentlemen over there and I are getting cold."

Orville stared condescendingly at his older brother. "Will, come on. This is history. People will be talking about this day for the rest of time. I'm sure we can take a moment to decide this. Historians will thank us later on."

"Fine," Wilbur said, taking a step back from their potential flying ship. Anything to get this process moving. What would you suggest?"

"Okay, Will. Hear me out. How about" he paused for effect, "*motorized glider*?

The scowl on Wilburt's face was enough to let his brother know of his disapproval.

"What's wrong with that?

"Well, technically, I see this as a step beyond gliders. If we do this, we need a different designation."

Orville rubbed his chin as he thought. Every few seconds he would offer up a suggestion: "Wooden bird?" "Flying carriage?" "Soaring stagecoach?"

Wilbur shook his head at each suggestion.

"I give up," Orville finally said. "Do you have an idea?"

"Well, there is the word the French use for their gliders that I've always liked."

"I thought you didn't like the word 'gliders.'"

"No, but their word doesn't have 'glider' in it. They use the word *aéroplane*, which is made up of *aero,* meaning 'air' and the Greek word *planos,* meaning 'wandering.'"

"Very well. We shall call it an air wanderer," Orville announced.

"Noooo. We're going to call it an airplane."

"An airplane?" Orville asked.

"Yes," his older brother proudly responded. "An Americanized version of their word. Yet, now it is ours. They won't be able to sue us about it."

"If you say so. From now on, all of these motorized flying crafts shall be called 'airplanes,'" the younger Orville announced. He then looked over at the group of men standing by a dune, pointed to it, and called out to them, "It's an airplane!"

He got no noticeable response back.

"Good. I'm glad that's settled," Wilbur said as he went back to checking the wires and controls.

"Whoa, whoa, whoa. Not so fast there, big brother. We still need to name this particular airplane before we fly it."

"What? Like a ship? Like the *U.S.S. Constitution*?"

"Exactly."

"Very well. I named it an airplane. You can decide on the name of our airplane since it will be the first in flight." He then added while looking at the blustery weather, "But hurry! This is taking all day."

Orville thought for a moment as the sand smacked him in the face. "How about 'the *Titanic*'? That would make a great name for a ship."

"Yes, it would. But that seems a little too grand for our spindly airplane. Let's let someone else have the good fortune of using that name down the road."

"The *Icarus*?"

"After the Greek who flew with wings created by his father?"

"Yes, that's the one."

"Doesn't he die in that fable?"

"Oh, right." He then thought a few more seconds and said, "The Wright Flyer."

Wilbur grinned as he repeated the name. "The Wright Flyer. I like that."

"Wright Flyer it is, then."

"Wonderful! Now, let's get those gentlemen over there to come over and help us turn our 'airplane,' so that we can take off."

"Take off? Take off what? Our coats? It's cold out here."

"It's just an expression, Orv. It means 'take off' from the ground."

"Whatever you say, big brother. But there's still one more thing."

"WHAT?"

"Don't get your long johns in a bunch. I just need to know the name of this place for the history books to record."

"They call this area 'Kill Devil Hills,'" Wilbur informed him.

"Ewww. We cannot have schoolchildren believing the first motorized manned flight took place at Kill Devil Hills."

An exasperated Wilbur threw up his hands and said, "Well, the town of Kitty Hawk is just down a couple of miles away. We can tell everyone that is where we first flew."

"Kitty Hawk," Orville said in admiration. "I like that. The "Hawk" blends in nicely with the flying."

"Good. Are you satisfied? Can we now strap you in and try this?

"Certainly, big brother," Orville said as he wriggled his way into the plane and onto his stomach so that he could handle the controls."

"Careful, little brother. Our airplane is very fragile."

"I am. I am. Still, this is very exciting. This shall be historic. And I hope that someday I shall be in the mile-high club."

"The what?" asked Wilbur.

"The mile-high club," answered Orville. "The mile-high club. Anyone who flies one mile up into the sky shall be a member of the 'mile-high club.'"

"Do you really think we shall one day be able to do that? To fly that high?"

"Certainly. We shall build large, sturdy airplanes and fly them higher and faster. Someday I hope that everyone shall be able to be in the mile-high club."

"Let's hope you're right, Orv. Let's hope you're right."

Chapter Ten

10

WINSTON CHURCHILL

GOBSMACKED AT DUNKIRK

"It's a bloody Brobdingnagian catastrophe! We're getting our arses kicked up and down northern France."

Neville Chamberlain watched as Winston Churchill, the new prime minister, angrily puffed on a cigar while glaring at his war cabinet.

"Perhaps if we gave Herr Hitler a call, I could appease his aggressiveness and hatred toward us?"

"Appease? Appease?" Churchill bellowed. "Is that your solution to everything? Because it bloody well did not work with the Sudetenland or Poland or Norway or France. What would you have me do, hand them the keys to Buckingham Palace?"

"Considering the circumstances we find ourselves in at Dunkirk, perhaps we should consider Neville's advice," offered Viscount Halifax.

"Oh shut up, Halifax," Churchill snapped. "I am not going to go beg for peace with that little German corporal as long as we have five hundred thousand men still fighting in France. In the last war it would have been simpler. We would have ordered the Aussies and Kiwis from New Zealand forward to attack the Huns while we got our people out. To England!"

"To England!" the war cabinet said in unison.

"And the rest of the United Kingdom," Colville mumbled to himself.

"But that's the point, my dear Winston," Chamberlain said. "They are not currently fighting. They are retreating."

"Retreating? Retreating, sir? I think not!" He then paused and looked around the room. "Very well, perhaps it is a retreat. But we should never call it that!"

"Then what should we call it, Prime Minister?" several voices asked.

"If I may," a voice from a dark corner of the room called out. It was Churchill's personal secretary, Jock Colville. "I have someone outside who may be of some help. An expert who deals exactly with this sort of thing."

"And what sort of thing would that be, young Colville?" the prime ministered inquired. "Battle tactics?"

"Retreat. Redeployment. We need to find the right way to present this to the population so as not to provoke panic."

"Really Mr. Colville, do you really think the peasants . . ."

"People," Colville interjected.

"People," Churchill continued. "Do you really think the people are close to panicking?"

Everyone at the table nodded with mumblings of "Quite so." "Undoubtedly." "Considering the circumstances, yes."

Churchill peered over his glasses to the personal secretary with his usual intimidating stare. "And what else can you tell me about this so-called 'expert'?"

"He is an American here on business, and I have asked him if he could provide us with a little of his expertise."

"An American?" Churchill bellowed. "Helping us? Why should we require an American's help?"

"Um, you're half American, Prime Minister," Colville replied.

"Oh, yes. Quite right. Quite right. Baseball. Apple pie. Coca-Cola. Obesity." Churchill continued, "What is this person's expertise in?"

"P.R., sir."

"P what?"

"Public relations. If you would allow me to bring him in. He can explain it all to you."

"Oh, very well. Send the man in."

Colville went to the door and opened it. Immediately, a blond-headed man in his mid-thirties rushed past him and directly to Churchill, whose hand he grabbed and shook vigorously before gushing, "What an honor, Prime Minister. What an honor. Boomer Vanderbilt here. No relation to the wealthy ones though. Ha ha. Wish I was though. I've heard so many great things about you from Jocko here."

He then proceeded to go around the desk and quickly shake hands with the members of the war cabinet before returning to stand next to the main person in the room.

"I have to tell you, it's just super to meet all of you here today."

"Yes, quite," Churchill replied with a wave his cigar. "Mr. Colville believes you might be of some help to us. To England."

"To England!" the cabinet said in unison.

"You betcha. To England," Boomer Vanderbilt added.

"And the rest of the United Kingdom," Colville mumbled to himself.

"First off, let me say, Mr. Prime Minister, I love the cigar. Very powerful. Very powerful. It's like waving a giant willy in front of these other gentleman to show your dominance."

"Willy?" Churchill looked bewilderedly at his cigar before him.

"Oh, sorry. Is that not what you call it here? What is the term you folks on the other side of the pond use? John Thomas, perhaps?"

He looked and pointed directly at Neville Chamberlain who, in a stunned panic, offered, "Todger?"

He then pointed to Halifax, who stuttered while saying, "Uh, uh, twig and berries?"

"Gentlemen. Gentlemen," a frustrated Churchill interrupted. "I believe we are getting off the subject."

"Absolutely right. Absolutely right, your prime ministership."

"What, pray tell, is it that you do, young man?" Halifax called up.

Vanderbilt abruptly put on a serious face as though deep in thought. "That is an excellent question, sir. Top-notch. Without a doubt. Obviously a group of very intelligent individuals here. England is very lucky to have you. To England!"

"To England!" the war cabinet said in unison.

"And the rest of the United Kingdom," Colville mumbled to himself.

"What I do is re-shape words. Smooth out messages. I make the unpleasant sound more palatable to your peasants."

"People," Colville interjected.

"People, yes," Vanderbilt repeated.

Churchill brought up his cigar to take another puff, but then decided against it after remembering the previous exchange. "So, what you are saying, sir? It sounds like very much like propaganda."

Vanderbilt's eyes went wide, and he waved his hands in mock horror. "Propaganda? No, no. The Nazi's do propaganda. What I do is public relations. Completely different. Totally different. Could not be more different."

"And how would you 'smooth out the message' for our current disaster?"

"Disaster? Are you kidding me? This is your finest hour."

“Finest hour? Are you mad, man?” Churchill blustered. “We’re in a massive retreat?”

The war cabinet grumbled, forcing the prime minister to say, “I mean, we are in a massive redeployment.”

“What do you hope to accomplish with this action, if I may inquire?” the American posed.

“We are hoping to get a portion of our army back so that we can fight another day should Herr Hitler decides he shall attempt to cross the channel and invade England.”

“To England!” the war cabinet said in unison.

“And the rest of the United Kingdom,” Colville mumbled to himself.

“So you are right. It’s not a retreat then,” Vanderbilt countered. “It is, in fact, an evacuation. And not just an evacuation, but a brave, heroic evacuation. An evacuation that will inspire millions of your compatriots as a huge success if you frame it correctly.”

A frustrated Chamberlain muttered to himself, “A brave, heroic evacuation where we leave all our tanks and guns back in France.”

Halifax leaned over to Chamberlain and declared, “I still say I can contact the Italians and have them broker a peace with the Germans for us. To Italy!”

The cabinet remained deathly quiet.

“Not happening, gentleman!” Churchill shouted.

“Hey, Winnie-baby,” Vanderbilt said as he smiled and patted the older man on the back. “Relax. Trust me on this. After all, I’m the one who convinced FDR to have his radio fireside chats to calm the American public during the Great Depression."

Churchill looked confused and mumbled to himself, "Winnie-baby?" He then leaned down to Chamberlain and whispered into his ear, "After this meeting, can I have this man taken out and shot?"

Chamberlain cleared his throat and whispered back, "Uh no, Winston, we don't do that sort of thing here."

"Humph. Pity." He then looked back toward the smiling P.R. man. "And what other thoughts do you have on the matter at hand?"

"Hmmm. What are you calling this campaign?"

"Operation Dynamo," answered Colville. "Admiral Ramsey came up with the name."

"Okay. Okay. Love it. Love it. 'Dynamo.' Very dynamic. Your audience will love it."

"My audience?" Churchill asked.

"Yes, the demographic group you are trying to hit," the American replied. "I mean, I don't have time to put together any focus groups to run the name up the flagpole to see if anyone salutes, but I have a gut feeling you have a winner with that one. That Ramsey sounds like he could have a future in public relations."

"Flagpole? Salute?" the puzzled prime minister asked.

"Exactly, now you're getting it," Vanderbilt said. "We need to find another hook though."

"Hook?"

"Yeah, something else that will make your audience care and want to buy in."

"Buy in?" Halifax asked. "As to the war, you mean?"

"Now you're cooking with gas," the P.R. man replied.

"Cooking with . . . ?" A confused Halifax stopped before finishing the question.

"It's their war too. You need their buy in to succeed." He stopped and thought a moment. "You just sent over the small, civilian ships with their owners, didn't you?"

"Yes," replied the prime minister. "But they are just a small part of the operation. They are mainly helping to ferry our soldiers from the shallow water where our big ships can't reach."

"Duck soup, then!"

"Duck what?"

"I'm telling you Prime Minister, this whole thing has been gift-wrapped for you with a pretty bow," he said beaming. "That is our hook. Everyday citizens sailing over their little boats to help the war effort. You make it sound like it was all them. They saved the day. Not the RAF or Royal Navy." He paused for effect. "It can't miss. Your finest hour!"

"Well, thank you, young man," Churchill replied. "We certainly will consider your recommendations."

As he headed to the door, Vanderbilt turned around and said, "Golden. I tell you it's golden. The people see themselves as a part of the war effort and the heroes in all this. That big palooka Adolf Hitler sure doesn't have any of his citizens floating around in little boats saving his soldiers."

"Yes, yes, thank you," Churchill called out as Boomer Vanderbilt went out and Colville closed the door.

"Palooka?" Halifax could be heard mumbling to himself. "The bloke is a complete wazzock. Totally barmy."

"I agree," chimed in Chamberlain. "I couldn't understand a word he said. Totally off the trolley. Complete codswallop. What a daft cow."

Colville now chimed in. "But do you think this, um, person, could be correct in his assessment?"

"Not for a bloody second," the great man replied. "The English people are much too intelligent to fall for any of that gobby American's mumbo jumbo manipulating them into feeling good about what's currently happening in France. To England!"

"To England!" the war cabinet said in unison.

"And the rest of the United . . . oh never mind," Colville mumbled to himself.

11

ADOLF HITLER

STRATEGIC PLANNING FOR THE THIRD REICH

"Ja, glad to see you all here today. Did everyone read my memo on why we're meeting?" Hitler looks around the room at his staff. "I can never tell if you are raising your hands or just saluting me." Laughter rises from the generals and other officers. "No, I joke, but seriously, we need to come up with a new system. If you do have a question, please use your left hand. I repeat, your left hand. Whenever you use your right hand, I end up saluting back half the time." More laughter breaks out.

"Okay, we're here to come up with a ten-year strategic plan to take over the world. Now, what we must first do is look at our core competencies. What do we do well? And, let's be honest here, what are some of our weaknesses? I'll start us off. Blaming everything on the Jews, we do well. Ja? Everyone agreed on that? But, and I am just being honest here, invading Russia, we could use some work on." Loud protestations erupt from the audience. "Nein, nein. I'm just keeping it real. That's how I am."

"Maybe we can blame the Russian campaign on the Jews," a voice from the back of the meeting room calls out. Laughter explodes out again.

Peering over his glasses and chuckling, Hitler said, "Goebbels. Leave it to you to come up with that one."

"It's my job, Mein Fuhrer."

"So it is. But this is a good start. Strengths and weaknesses. Anybody? Just call them out. Let's start with strengths."

A voice calls out, "Aryan purity."

"Ja. Good." Hitler nods to his secretary to write it down.

"German organization," another calls out from the back.

"Okay. But that reminds me. While I have you all here. I have a question about an invoice that came across my desk a few days ago for patches to be worn by . . . What are we calling them now? Voluntary Recreation Centers? Is that it?"

"Sorry, Mein Fuehrer. What Centers?" a voice calls out.

“Come on, guys. You know. Those places we send our ‘special’ citizens. The ones not Aryan or the ‘correct’ religion. You know what I’m talking about.”

“Ahhh.” The officer all nod knowingly.

“Good. So, I have a question about the patches to be worn by the *volunteers* at the Voluntary Rec Centers,” he looks around the room to see more nodding. “Now I understand the charges for the Star of David patches for the Juden. And the pink ones for the funny boys. But what are these grayish brown ones for?”

A man stands up in the front row. “I think I can answer that one, Mein Fuehrer.”

“Ah, Himmler. Ja. You have the answer?”

“Ja, Mein Fuehrer. That’s for the *volunteers,*” he pauses for effect, “with the peanut allergies.”

“Peanut allergies? You’ve got to be pulling my leg, Heinrich.”

“Nein, Mein Fuehrer. It is a Health Department regulation. There might be nuts in the food for the other *volunteers*, so we need to keep those with the peanut allergies away from them. We did not do it at first, and I got a fifty mark fine. So now we are in compliance.”

Hitler nods. “Ja. Okay. I can see that. We Germans love our rules, which is why we should be rulers of the world. Am I right?”

Big laugh and applause from the audience.

“Of course, I wish we had thought of that before we opened these places up. Voluntary Recreation Centers? That has always sounded a little weak to me. No one in his right mind would buy that. Not even Churchill. But if we had said we were putting these people here to protect them from the general population because of peanut allergies, we would have come out looking like the good guys." Sighs. "Ach well, live and learn."

Suddenly, a hand rose up from the end of the table and a voice called out, "Mein Fuehrer, I have a question."

"Certainly, young man," he replied, peering over his glasses. "And you are?"

"Oberleutnant Günter Kronberger, Mein Fuehrer."

He leaned down to Goebbels, who whispered in his ear, "Eva Braun's second cousin."

"Ah, ja," he said as he leaned back up and smiled. "Young Kronberger, of course. You have a question?"

"Ja, Mein Fuehrer."

"Good. Good. We are very open to questions here. No such thing as a bad question. We welcome them all in a free and open environment. Don't we, mein coworkers."

They all nodded enthusiastically in agreement.

"Well, Mein Fuehrer. I just think we may be fighting this war with one arm tied behind our backs."

"How so?" Hitler asked quizzically with a raised eyebrow and his little mustache twitching to one side, which made him look a little like Charlie Chaplin, but everyone had the good sense not to laugh.

"Well, I mean, we have many of our top scientists locked up in the concen . . . I mean, Voluntary Recreation Centers. Couldn't we use their talents in the war effort? Not to mention the carpenters and bakers and doctors and such there who could aid us greatly in our noble fight?"

There was a moment of stunned silenced as Goebbel's and Himmler's eye grew wide in shocked amazement, while those sitting by Kronberger quietly scooted their chairs away from him the little they could.

Hitler maintained his composure as he replied with another smile, "You bring up a very good point, Oberleutnant. But I'm afraid it may be too big of a topic to tackle here today. Why don't you write up a report and bring it back to me in, say, a week with your recommendations, and then we shall take them on."

"Ja, Mein Fuhrer. I will do just that," replied the grinning and enthusiastic young officer.

"Look forward to reading it. Look forward to reading it," Hitler replied, still smiling. He then leaned down to Goebbels and whispered, "After this meeting, have the young oberleutnant taken out back and shot."

"You got it, Mein Fuhrer," Goebbels whispered back, while he and Hitler continued to smile down the table at the eager young man.

12

JOSEF STALIN

WE THE PEASANTS IN ORDER TO FORM A MORE PERFECT SOVIET UNION

The new driver took extra care as he drove down the streets of Kuybyshev on his way to the temporary Soviet capital building. Being a resident of the city, he had been picked for this job because of his familiarity with the local streets. Between being extra cautious not to run over the motorcycle escort in front of him to concern about the absolute safety of his passenger, he had greater worries than an invasion by the ruthless German army.

Suddenly a car cut him and the two motorcycles in front of him off, causing them all to slam on their brakes, before it disappeared just as quickly down a side street. A look of terror came upon him as he looked into the rearview mirror to check on his companion.

"I am so sorry, Comrade Stalin. He came out of nowhere and swerved right in front of us. Do you want me to tell the escort to go after him and arrest him?"

"Arrest him? Nyet. The poor man may have been in a rush to get home because he had diarrhea or some other intestinal distress," the leader of the Soviet Union replied. "Kindness and patience. Two virtues the Communist Party is known for."

"Da, Comrade," he replied while waving to the escort to resume their journey. "Kindness and patience. Very good." And he put the car back in gear before continuing on, soon coming up to a group of soldiers pointing their bayonets at a handful of babushka women who unenthusiastically waved and tossed a couple of mostly dead flowers at the car.

"Da. They love their Uncle Joe. The power of the Slavic people is in the strength and determination of their women. I am a beloved figure to the people."

"Peasants," his driver corrected him.

"Da. Beloved figure to the peasants. Spasiba."

They drove a little further and spotted three people standing in front of a can with a fire in it. One was feeding books to the flames and then warming his hands.

"Excellent," Stalin said in a cheery voice. "Probably doing the party's work by burning some bourgeois capitalist books. If I had time, I would give them each a medal, but, alas, I must get to my office to serve the people."

"Peasants."

"Da. Peasants."

The driver did his best to avoid potholes and make it as smooth a ride as possible lest he be sent to fight at Stalingrad with his brothers. With every bump he would wince and look back at his leader, who never seemed to notice but instead would comment on what a lovely day it was, how pretty the clouds were, and how the weather was warming.

"What is your name, Comrade Driver?" Stalin asked nonchalantly at one point.

"Um, I do not have one. My political officer has not assigned me a name yet."

"I understand," Stalin replied. He then leaned forward. "I'll let you in on a little secret, Comrade Driver. I was not born Josef Stalin. I was born Ioseb Besarionis dze Jughashvili. But that is quite a mouthful, and Josef Stalin it is now."

They drove a few more blocks when the leader of the Soviet Union saw a group of young schoolchildren walking along on the sidewalk, being ushered by a stern-looking schoolmaster.

"Pull over. Pull over," he said enthusiastically.

The driver complied, as did the motorcycle escort. Rolling down his window, Stalin beckoned to the children to come over. The humorless teacher was about to chide the children and the man in the car until he looked closer, and all the blood drained from his face.

"Comrade! Comrade! Uncle Joe!" the children called out as he reached out to shake their hands and stroke their faces before waving and having the driver continue on down the gray streets.

"Education is a weapon, whose effect depends on who holds it in his hands and at whom it is aimed," he said mostly to himself.

After another two blocks, the driver again slammed on the brakes as he thought he heard an airplane overhead and knew from past experience it was more likely to be the enemy's than theirs.

His rider cocked his head, looked out the window, and smiled. "Be calm my young comrade. Do not be so jumpy. It is nothing."

"I'm sorry, Comrade. It's just that they seem to be getting closer and closer. Should we arm the citizens and send them out?"

"We don't let them have ideas. Why would we let them have guns? The hated Germans may look like they are currently doing well, but history has shown there are no invincible armies. Let them come into the maw of the mighty bear so that it may shut upon them and not allow them to escape. Our way is the right way. Not the stupid Americans or silly British."

"But they are helping us, aren't they, Comrade?"

"They think are, but do not worry, young man. Our way is superior—in politics as in battle. Remember, people who cast the votes decide nothing. The people who count the votes decide everything. After this war is over and we have defeated the Germans, we shall set our sights upon the capitalistic usurpers. History teaches us that the class or social group that plays the principal role in social production and performs the main functions in production must, in the course of time, inevitably take control of that production. So we shall have control of the production and, therefore, the control of the world."

"Thank you, Comrade. I shall remember that."

At last, they pulled up in front of the nondescript, gray administrative building currently serving as the center of the government. The driver got out and went around the car to open the door for his passenger. Stalin got out, looked up at the sky, then back at his driver, to whom he nodded and smiled his appreciation.

Striding confidently through the double doors, which were again being held open by his driver, he made his way across the lobby to a small, brown wooden desk. A young woman of about twenty looked up. Upon realizing who was before her, she stood up, unsmiling and implacably serious.

"Ah, Comrade Zariyah, what a pleasure it is to see you." He then leaned over and kissed each of her cheeks.

"Da, Comrade. It is a pleasure to see you as well," she said with a dull, lifeless look in her eyes as she stared past him.

"Da. You are a flower, Comrade." He then turned to his driver to announce, "Gaiety is the most outstanding feature of the Soviet Union."

The man nodded quickly in response.

He then turned back to the young Russian woman before him. "And how is that charming mother of yours?"

"She is well considering. She currently has pneumonia because our communal apartment has no heat. Still, we are bravely bearing up." She stuck out her sexless chest in dour pride as she spoke.

"Excellent. Excellent. Well, give her my best. I'm happy to hear the peop. . . I mean, peasants, are doing so well," as he moved past her and the broken elevator and up the stairway to his enormous office. He beckoned his driver to follow him up. "Come. Come. I may have use for you a little later."

Immediately upon entering the cavernous office, he sat down behind his Brobdingnagian desk and lit his pipe. After he took a couple of puffs, he calmly called out, "Very well. Let it begin."

In came a tiny bespectacled middle-aged sour-looking man wearing a dark, wrinkled suit.

"Good morning, Comrade," he said as he bowed, the pile of papers in his arms nearly falling out.

"Good morning, Comrade Sidorov," Stalin replied. "And how goes things this morning."

The man looked down nervously. "I am sorry to bring you bad news first thing in the morning, Comrade, but there has been as setback."

"A setback? That's a shame," the placid Stalin replied.

"Da. Information is spotty, but SMERSH reports that 168th Rifle Division was overrun by a German Panzer Corps yesterday about twenty kilometers southwest of Stalingrad. Half of them were killed or captured. The other half fled safely to our lines."

"It takes a brave man to be a coward in the Red Army," he replied to his assistant. He then turned and smiled to his driver. "You see. I was right. I already have a job for you."

The young man stood immediately.

"I want you to drive all the way to Stalingrad. Find General Zhukov. Tell him I said he is to execute those survivors of the 168th or 169th or whichever Rifle Division it was as an example to all others who chose to run in the face of our enemy."

The young man nodded and then turned sharply and quickly left the room.

Josef Stalin then clapped his hands together and said to his assistant, "Now that that is done, what am I having for breakfast?"

13

NIKOLA TESLA

MY HEART TAKES WING

The nattily dressed Nikola Tesla left his Hotel New Yorker room and rode thirty-three floors down the elevator to the lobby where he heard a radio blaring from behind the concierge's desk.

"Yes, that's mine," he immediately thought to himself, as he did every day whenever he heard a newscast, a ball game, or Jack Benny's voice coming from a box. "My invention. Mine. Not Marconi. Mine. Mine. Mine. Check the patents, Guglielmo, you Fascist babbler. Supporting Mussolini and his flock of friends. "

He migrated his way over to the Garment District through the Theater District on his daily migration to

Central Park. Along the way, noticing as he always did, the electric signs in the stores hawking their wares and along the street, even the streetlights and giant theater marquees and neon lamps, which had been darkened because of the war. Still, he knew his part. They were working because of him and his invention of alternating current electricity. "Oooo, I'm direct current. I can only move slowly in one direction," he would often mumble to himself during his walks. 'Yeah, where did that get you, Edison? *Idi do djavola.*"

After about thirty minutes, he arrived at his favorite bench in Central Park, which he circled three times before sitting down, all the while still mumbling, "Thomas Edison. Thomas Edison. Thomas Edison. Thinks he is the cock of the walk. Everybody loves Thomas Edison. Mickey Rooney played him in a movie. Big deal. Someday Hollywood will get Clark Gable to play Nikola Tesla. Or Gary Cooper. Or maybe even Cary Grant. Then everyone will know what a big deal I was and still am."

He tapped the armrest three times and then his foot three times. He looked across to the trees and down the sidewalk. But as he turned his head, he suddenly noticed she was next to him on the bench.

"Right on time as always," he said smiling, his cranky mood immediately evaporating.

"As are you," she replied. "Looking dapper and resplendent as always. Your usual fine feather."

"Well, I always want to look my best for you. If that means a little extra preening, well, you deserve it."

"Oh, Nikola," she cooed. "You flatter me."

Tesla looked up at the sky and the rolling white clouds before looking to the ground and saying, "He killed an elephant. And he didn't just kill it; he purposely murdered it. And he didn't just murder it; he tortured it in the most inhumane way possible."

"Poor Topsy," she agreed. "Yes, Edison was a monster. He also electrocuted dogs, cats, cattle, and horses just to squawk about how he was being treated unfairly and how his direct current was superior."

"No, the greedy vulture did it to try and make more money. As if he didn't already have enough. Always robbin' me."

"And some of that money was rightfully yours. I know."

He moved his hand and raised her head. "You understand me better than anyone."

Just then an older, well-dressed woman walked past, pausing to stare at them before continuing on.

"What are you looking at, you old hen," Nikola growled and as he pointed at the woman. "What's the matter? Haven't you ever seen a genius before?"

"Now, Nikola," his companion said. "I'm sure the woman was just surprised to see someone who looked so happy in these trying times."

"I suppose," he groused. "If only the United States military would allow me, I would develop my TeleForce, which could shoot down Nazi planes before they could get anywhere near their target. It would end all war. But no, instead they snipe at me, make fun of my idea and call it a death ray. It is not a death ray. It is more of a focused-energy fence that would prevent war machines and soldiers from crossing it and attacking another country to poach their resources."

She snuggled a little closer to him. "Yes, my dear Nikola. I know it is a bitter pill to swallow."

As she moved closer to him, his eagle eyes spotted a man in a dark coat, black hat, and sunglasses about thirty feet away from them, standing next to a bush and just staring off into space. "You see. You see. That man over there by the Duck Oak tree. He follows me all the time. FBI. They make fun of my ideas and inventions, but they make sure I do not talk to any possible enemy agents. My guess is those turkeys are waiting for me to die soon so that they can rummage through my room and take all my papers. They will then parrot back my ideas to the public and claim they were their inventions and not mine. They think I am ravin' mad, but I am not a loon."

"I have known many cuckoos in my life, and you are certainly not one," she agreed.

"They act as though all my inventions were done as a lark when I was truly trying to help mankind. I would never say a word to any of our country's enemies."

"Not a peep, I'm sure," she said.

"You would think they would have begged me for help. After all, it is the Tesla Coil. It is the Tesla Turbine. It is not the Henry Ford Coil or George Westinghouse

Turbine. They are named after me because I am the one who invented them. Most scientist are too chicken to invent the things I did. The magnifying transmitter, the shadowgraph, hydroelectric power, induction motor. Even the radio-controlled boat that I used to scare the geese with. These were all mine. If Max Planck had invented any of these, he would crow about it from the highest rooftop. Think of the millions I should have been paid."

"It would have provided a tidy nest egg. That's for sure."

He looked at her and smiled broadly as he reached over and stroked the back of her head three times.

"Oh, Nikola. Such boldness! What will people think of me for allowing such forwardness in a public park? They will think I am some hotsy totsy little chickadee."

"They will think no such thing" he reassured her.

"Still," she said. "It is time for me to go and you to head back to your hotel."

"Must you go?" he asked. "I do so miss your company. I have never known anyone like you. It's as though we were meant for each other."

"Now, Nikola. You know it would never work out between us."

"But why? You understand me so. Give me one good reason as to why we could not have a relationship."

"Because, my dear Nikola," she cooed. "You are a human being, and I am but a pigeon." And with that, she spread her wings and took flight until the next time they would meet.

14

IKE, JOSEPH MCCARTHY, AND LIBERACE

THESE HAPPY DAYS ARE YOURS AND MINE

Howard Cunningham stood at the foot of the stairs of their comfortable middle-class Milwaukee home; his wife, Marion, sat in a chair in the living looking straight down at the floor, dabbing a tear in her eye with a tissue, as he called up, "Kids! Come on downstairs! Family meeting!"

Richie and Joanie came bounding down just as they had done a thousand times in their years living there in their ideal Midwestern existence.

"What's up, Dad?" Richie asked.

"Yeah, Dad. Is something wrong?" his sister chimed in.

"Here. Just sit down on the couch so we can discuss it," he replied, waving his arm in the direction of the living room and then standing by his wife, who did not look up.

"Wait," Joanie said as she sat down. "If this is a family meeting, shouldn't Chuck be here?"

Their mother stifled a sob, causing her children to look over at her in alarm.

"I'm afraid I have some very bad news," their father said in his most paternal way.

"Wait! Is Chuck all right? Has he been in wreck or something?" Joanie asked, the panic in her voice becoming obvious.

"Yes. Well, no," her father answered. "Something has come up. Something serious. Very serious, I'm afraid."

"Dad, spit it out," Richie said, showing the concern on his face, his red, thinning hair starting to bead with sweat.

"All right. You know how our senator for Wisconsin, Joseph McCarthy, has been rooting out communists in the government and society?" Howard asked.

"You mean Chuck is a communist!" Richie said aghast. "I refuse to believe it."

"No. No. Your brother is not a communist," his father replied. "At least, we don't think so. The two may be combined in some way. I'm not sure."

"Two what?" Richie asked.

"Do you know about President Eisenhower signing Executive Order 10450 a couple of years ago?"

His children shook their heads no as Joanie asked, "What is that?"

"Well, you've heard of the Red Scare in government?" They both nodded. "Have you heard of the Lavender Scare in government and society?" He then turned to his forlorn wife, and said, "Maybe this isn't an appropriate topic for Joanie. Perhaps she should leave the room."

"Dad! I've heard about homosexuality!" Joanie snorted. "I'm not a child."

"You have?" her disturbed father asked ashast. "How? Certainly not in schools."

"From Jenny Piccalo, of course. She has a cousin she says is a 'Nancy Boy.'"

"Nancy Boy. Can we say that?" Howard asked.

"Considering the era we live in," Joanie responded, "that might be one of the nicer euphemisms Jenny could use."

"Still, what does that have to do with Chuck? Surely he isn't one," Richie countered.

"I'm afraid so," Howard said as Marion stifled another sob. "Chuck's ROTC unit in college, as part of Ike's Executive Order 10450, had to check on the personal lives of everyone in the program. We refused to believe it ourselves, but they have not only kicked him out of ROTC but his fraternity and the college as well. Your mother and I confronted him about it, and he admitted it is true."

"Then where is he?" Richie demanded to know as he stood. "He's family. Shouldn't we be there for him? Supporting him?"

Finally, their mother spoke up. "It's the 1950s. It's Milwaukee."

"Your mother is right. There are no homosexuals in the 1950s and certainly not in Milwaukee."

"Dad, Liberace is from Milwaukee," Richie pointed out.

"Liberace is not a homosexual."

"Dad!?!? Come on!" a stunned Richie responded.

"He's flamboyant. There's a difference. Show biz people are expected to be flashy."

"Montgomery Clift?"

"Rumor."

"Rock Hudson?"

"Rumor."

"Tab Hunter?"

"Just a rumor."

"And yet you believe it about our brother, Chuck?"

"As I said, because he admitted it to us. He said he's been hiding it for some time."

Marion dabbed a handkerchief to her eye and said, "I blame myself. I should never have let him play a squirrel in that third grade play."

"That was me that played the squirrel in the school play, Mom," Richie pointed out.

She stared at him for a moment, eyeing him over, and contemplating before adding, "Nevertheless, I was too smothering. I encouraged him to read. Color pictures. Join the Boy Scouts. It's my fault."

Howard went over and patted her on the shoulder, "Now, now Marion. It's not your fault. If it's anyone's fault, it's mine. I should have played catch with him more in the backyard instead of spending countless evenings trying to build the hardware store into a success."

"Well," Richie interrupted. "I don't know how it works. Playing catch more. Reading too much. I do know that he was never as interested in the pictures of the native women in the *National Geographic* magazines Dad would leave around for us to find."

"You're saying Dad never explained the birds and the bees to Chuck and Richie and just left magazines around for them to learn stuff from?" an astonished Joanie asked.

"It's the 1950s. It's Milwaukee," her mother replied.

"Speaking as the smug, moral compass of the family, I'm not sure what the big deal is." Richie pointed out. "After all, we have never expressed any particular religious affiliation. For all I know, we may be part of sect that is okay with homosexuality."

"It's the 1950s. It's Milwaukee," his mother replied.

"Your mother is right. It doesn't matter what religion we are or aren't. It is the 1950s and this is Milwaukee.

We cannot have a homosexual in the family. We cannot ever speak about him or acknowledge his existence ever again."

"That seems a little harsh," Joanie said.

"We're doing this for your protection and ours. Kids would bully you at school. My hardware business would be ruined. If your mother belonged to any civic organizations or women's groups, she would be kicked out immediately and ostracized."

"Do you really think people would act that way?" Joanie asked.

"It's the 1950s. It's Milwaukee," her mother replied.

"Hold on. Hold on. Hold on." Richie said in a flash of inspiration. "I think I may have a solution. You know how Fonzie can hit a jukebox or a television or an engine and make them work? Maybe we could have him punch Chuck and fix him and make him a heterosexual."

"Yes," Joanie declared in agreement. "And then, we could have Fonzie go around the country punching homosexuals and straightening them all out and converting them."

Howard paused to consider the suggestion for a moment. "I'm not convinced that would work. Plus, I'm not sure I want Fonzie around Chuck."

"Why not?" Richie asked.

"I just have a funny feeling about Fonzie. I mean, look at it. He has date after date after date with all these beautiful women. Yet, he cannot seem to ever have a lasting relationship that goes more than one or two days.

Haven't you ever wondered why that is? Plus, the man does seem to be into grooming and preening more than most real men. And he also seems to have a great fondness of leather clothing. I mean, have you ever heard him mention that he likes John Wayne or Charlton Heston movies? The signs are there."

Richie and Joanie looked at each other in disbelief.

"If Chuck is lavender, and Fonzie could be lavender, does that mean there's anyone we can trust to be truly not lavender?" Richie asked.

"Arnold? Ralph Malph and Potsie Weber?" Joanie asked.

"Ralph and Potsie are nerds. They're not homosexuals," Ritchie refuted. "Arnold? He's a life-long bachelor. It's the 1950s. It's Milwaukee. I have no idea."

"So do you plan to keep Chuck locked in his room for the rest of his life? Are we supposed to ignore him?" Joanie asked her parents.

"No. Chuck has already moved out," her father responded.

"What?" Rich and Joanie said in shocked unison.

"Without even saying goodbye?" Joanie shrieked.

"We thought it was for the best to make a clean break."

"Well, where did he go?" Richie demanded.

"He said he was going to head out to San Francisco. He has an old basketball buddy who lives out there and works as a yoga instructor—whatever that is."

"Can we go visit him someday?" Joanie asked.

"No. Certainly not," her father snapped.

"Why not?"

"We asked our friend, Garry. Garry Marshal. And he said we were to never mention your brother ever again."

"Isn't Garry Marshal Italian?" Richie asked.

"It's the 1950s. It's Milwaukee. He can't be Italian, unless he works in the restaurant industry like Al," his mother answered.

"And we're to do everything this Garry Marshal tells us," Richie asked sarcastically.

"Yes. We are," his father replied. "From this point on, we never mention Chuck Cunningham ever again. He no longer exists."

"Just like that?" Richie asked.

"Just like that," his father responded.

Suddenly, Marion jumped to her feet and said, "Okay, who's ready for some pot roast?"

"Pot roast, Mom?" Richie asked. "You think we should just forget everything and pot roast will take care of it?"

"It's the 1950s. It's Milwaukee," his mother replied.

"Great," their father said with too much enthusiasm. "Now, who's going to help your mother in the kitchen cook the pot roast? Everyone loves her pot roast."

"Especially Chuck," mumbled Joanie.

"Shhhhh," her father said. "Do not say his name."

A stunned Richie shook his head and slowly said, "Pot roast. Sure. I guess. It's just a lot to take in right now."

His father clapped his hands together and said, "Great. Let's go." And headed toward the kitchen with his son and wife.

"I'll be there in a minute," Joanie called out to them as they left the room. She then went to the phone and dialed. "Hello, Mrs. Piccalo. . . . It's Joanie Cunningham. Is Jennie there? . . . Hello, Jennie. It's Joanie. Look, we're going to have to cool it with the experimentation for a while. . . . I'll explain later."

15

ALBERT EINSTEIN

THEORIZING ABOUT ENTANGLEMENT

Shuffling around his Princeton, New Jersey, home in his worn slippers, Albert Einstein went into his study and found his favorite pipe beneath a mountain of papers on his desk. He tapped it in the palm of his hand and considered sitting down in the chair. What he had planned was of upmost importance, and he needed a quiet place in which to work and, for the professor, thinking was work. No, he would be too distracted here. This problem needed his undivided attention, and he knew he if he tried to tackle it at his desk, he would end up looking at the papers and letters strewn about in front of him.

He moved into the living room, its curtains drawn. It was dark. It was quiet. There were books piled up on the floor and every table, but nothing that would catch his eye and take him away from what he intended.

He settled into his favorite easy chair, still clutching his pipe, but not lighting it. It was here that the experiment would begin. He planned to conduct one of his favorite thought experiments, just as he had done in 1905 when he imagined he was on a train going the speed of light to help him create his understanding of special relativity. Today was the day he would get Niels Bohr off his back. Today was the day he had put aside to unify quantum mechanics with quantum entanglement —or disprove entanglement.

Oh, who was he trying to kid? He was there to prove the supremacy of quantum mechanics over quantum entanglement. "Quantum entanglement. I still say it is spooky action at a distance," he mumbled to himself. "God does not play dice with the universe."

He moved around until he was comfortable in his chair and mumbled to himself, "After all, Schrödinger, his cats, and I invented quantum mechanics, all you jerks in the scientific world."

Sitting back, he closed his eyes. *Think, Albert. Think.* He paused as he considered what he should think about. *I'm on a train going from one particle to another across the universe. How can I arrive there simultaneously? Faster than the speed of light?* He opened his eyes and shook his head. *Nein, that is ridiculous.* He closed his eyes shut again. *What is it I am trying to do? Multiple particles are linked together in a way such that the measurement of one particle's quantum state determines the possible quantum states of the other particles. Ergo, in mein mind, I must picture these particles. Here and, let us say, Uranus.*

With his eyes tightly shut, he began to picture protons, electrons, and neutrons spinning all around in front of him. But then a strange thing happened. More atoms joined. And more and more. It was becoming a shape. A shape of . . . a woman?

"Hello, Albert."

"Ach du leiber, what are you doing here?"

"Oh, Albert. I have always wanted to meet you."

Standing before him, as if she really were there, was the image of the world's most famous sex symbol, Marilyn Monroe, wearing a white, low-cut, form-fitting gown.

"Miss Monroe. What in Newton's name are you doing here?"

"Why, Albert. I came to help you," she said breathlessly. "And please call me Marilyn. It sounds so sexy with your accent."

"But why you, eeh, Marilyn? Why would my subconscious conjure up you? Shouldn't it be Max Planck or Werner Heisenberg or Boris Podolsky or . . .?"

"Because, Albert," Marilyn interrupted. "I'm the one you think about the most."

"Dat is not true!"

Marilyn lowered her head and smiled coyly. "Now, Albert."

"Well, well, I would not describe it as 'thinking' about you. It's more like, like, like . . ."

"Fantasizing?"

"I am a world-renowned physicist, madam. I do not 'fantasize.' I theorize."

"Whatever you say, Herr 'Theoretical' Physicist." She smiled demurely and asked, "What shall we theorize about? I have some postulations." And she took a step closer to him.

Nein. Nein. Nein. Nein. Nein. Wake up, Albert. Wake up. With a violent jerk, his eyes opened wide to an empty, dark room. He was in a cold sweat and breathing heavily. He looked down and saw that he had snapped his pipe in two.

His first effort had been an absolute disaster—the Hindenburg Disaster of thought experiments. He took a deep breath, determined to make another attempt. Leaning back in his chair, he closed his eyes. *Try, try again. If at first you don't succeed.* He steadied his breathing. *And do not think of Marilyn. Do not think about Marilyn. Do not think about Marilyn.*

"What do you mean, 'Do not think about Marilyn'?"

There she was. Standing before him once again. This time wearing a white, one-piece bathing suit. She looked down at herself. "Albert, why do you have me dressed up like Betty Grable now?"

Albert shrugged. "I have a type."

"It's a little tight. Don't you think?"

"Nein. Nein. Nein. I am not going to think about you. I am not going to think about you. I am going to concentrate on the problem at hand."

"Which is?"

"Which is quantum entanglement." He stopped and said, "Wait. Why am I explaining this to you?"

"Are you, Albert? Or are you explaining it to yourself?"

"I am ignoring you. You are merely a figment of my imagination."

"But what a great imagination you have!"

"Ya," Albert replied smiling, as he looked the blonde movie star up and down approvingly. "I have to concur with that one."

"Schrödinger used thought experiments to come up with his dead cat!" She paused. "Or was it alive?

"It was both, actually. At the same time."

"Did he come up with it by himself during his 'theorizing'?"

"There's a rumor that Greta Garbo was the one he, uh, saw."

"So, I can help?" she giggled as she jumped up and down.

The professor followed her with his eyes as she leapt in elation, inwardly knowing he was enjoying the spectacle far too much. Plus, it was making his neck hurt.

"Nein. Nein. Nope. No siree, Bob. Back to work. Back to my real ladylove, physics."

Marilyn stopped jumping, lowered her head, and pouted at the brilliant sitting man. "Aren't you the one who said, 'When you sit with a pretty girl for two hours, you think it's only a minute, but when you sit on a hot stove for a minute, you think it's two hours. That's relativity.'" She then tweaked his nose playfully and purred, "How long do you think we have been here together? One minute or two hours? Relatively speaking. You have a pretty girl before you. What is time in relation to that?"

"I have a particle with me here in New Jersey," he said, ignoring her. "It has a companion particle on Uranus. . ."

"On my what?" Marilyn giggled.

Einstein muttered, "I knew I should have said Jupiter."

"Uranus. That's such a silly name. Don't you think, Albert."

She moved to him and sat down on an arm of his chair.

"Well, ja, now that you mention it. I suppose they could have named it something a little less naughty. You know, Marie Curie also used to always giggle whenever someone said 'Uranus.'"

She began twirling a strand of his wild unkempt hair in her fingers. "Really, Albert. Does it have to be today that you work on this problem? It's been a mystery to physicists for decades."

Albert Einstein looked at the figure sitting next to him and then up to her face. He sighed. "Perhaps you are correct. So what if I can't figure this out. There will be other smart people coming along. Maybe they will have the answer."

With that he smiled and pulled Marilyn onto his lap. She nestled her head on his shoulder. "I'm glad you are at peace with that."

"Ja, and if I do not ever get it figured out, perhaps I will just start a rumor that I had an affair with you to distract everyone from thinking about it."

"I'm very happy to be your quantum entanglement," Marilyn whispered into his ear. She then pulled away slightly, looked him in the eye and pointed out, "But Albert, you do understand that I am not real, don't you? You're not actually making love with the physical Marilyn Monroe.

"Ja," Albert said as he pulled her imaginary head back to rest on his shoulder. "But the world doesn't have to know that."

16

WALT DISNEY

BIBBIDI-BOBBIDI-EWWWW

Vigorously crushing another butt into the already half-filled ashtray, Walt Disney hurriedly picked up his third pack that morning and lit another cigarette, taking a long drag until the faded blue intercom box to the right of him buzzed and a woman's voice called out, "Mr. Disney, your nine o'clock appointment is here. A Mr. Fanucci."

Pushing down the button, he responded, "Thank you, Dolly. Please send him in."

Getting up from his office chair, he went to the door and shook hands with the short, nattily dressed, dark-haired man carrying a binder under his left arm who entered.

"Mr. Funicello, welcome," he said as he guided the gentleman to one of the two green chairs in front of his Brobdingnagian desk before returning to his own chair.

"That's Fanucci," the man corrected him as he looked around the office filled with portraits of Mickey Mouse, Donald Duck, Snow White, and other Disney cartoon characters.

"Oh, yes, yes, of course, of course," the tycoon replied as he brought the cigarette up to his mouth once again. "Well, let's get to it. I see you brought what I assume to be are catalogs with your products?"

Before the man could answer, the intercom buzzed once again and the same woman's voice said, "Mr. Disney, your brother, Roy, is here. Were you expecting him?"

He tapped his cigarette ash into the ashtray before pressing the button and replying, "Yes, that's fine. It's good that he's here. Please send him in, Dolly."

But this time he did not rise and greet the person coming into the room. Instead, he simply smiled and nodded as his brother made his way to the remaining chair and sat down, all the while fumbling with the pile of folders in his arms.

"Roy, I want you to meet Mr. Funicello."

"Fanucci," the man said to Roy as he leaned over to shake his hand.

The elder Disney brother nodded his head while shaking the man's hand and said, "Don't worry. He does that to ever Italian-American person he meets. He thinks you're all named Funicello."

Walt glared at Roy through the haze of cigarette smoke hovering over his desk before saying to the man, "Oh, he's just exaggerating. I assure you." He then turned his attention back to his brother. "Mr. Fannuciello is here to show me some freezers he has in his appliance store in Anaheim."

The man nodded as he opened up his binder, which had pictures and pages of specs throughout. "I brought what we have, but I am a little confused. Are you wanting an industrialized freezer for use in the park or something smaller for your home?"

"Smaller. Definitely smaller. It is for my personal use."

The man scanned the office before asking," For here or your home?"

"Here. In the park, I mean. Not industrial size, but it needs to be fairly large."

The salesman pulled out a photo and papers and said, "Well, this is our Model A202, which is eight cubic feet and can fit almost an entire side of beef with room for your other frozen items." He placed in onto the Brobdingnagian desktop and slid it over to famous man who took the time to place his cigarette down in the ashtray before looking over the information.

"Well, I'm not a freezer expert, Mr. Finnochio. How many pounds would that hold?"

"About eight-five to one hundred, Mr. Disney."

"Hmmm, no." Walt quietly answered. "I'm looking for something a little bigger than that."

The man took out another picture and papers and said, "Well, there is the Model A260, which is about twelve cubic feet. That easily holds two hundred pounds of beef with room for other items, depending, of course, on how the beef is cut."

"Cut? No. I'm not planning on having anything cut. My question is, 'How long is it? Can you lay a person down lengthwise in it?"

A bewildered Mr. Fanucci and Roy looked at each other in panic before Roy chimed in, "Walt, what in the Wonderful Wide World of Disney are you asking? Are you still mad at Tommy Kirk about the marijuana arrest? Because this is NOT the answer. We're a family studio."

"No, no, no," a laughing Walt replied. "It's nothing like that. It's for me."

"You?" the salesman asked. "You want to lay an entire cow lengthwise in it?"

Taking another drag on his cigarette, the legendary man said, "No. I mean it is for me me. I'm the one who will be lengthwise in it."

A still-confused Roy said, "You've lost me, Walt. What is this all about?"

Stamping out his latest cigarette and lighting a new one, the younger brother answered, "Like I said, it's for me. You see, I am not getting any younger and we still have lots of work to do with our upcoming movies and Epcot Center and such. Should something unforeseen happen," he paused and took a long drag, "and I should pass away, I want to be frozen and—when they have found a cure for whatever I may have died from—be thawed and continue our work."

"But Mr. Disney, my freezers were not made for such a use. I don't think you can, can, can . . ."

"He's right, Walt," the other Disney chimed in. "From what I've heard about this process, it doesn't work this way. It is still very much experimental. We can't stuff you into a freezer when you die and thaw you out like you are a Thanksgiving turkey."

"Not to mention there is something unholy about the whole thing," the salesman mumbled to himself.

"Oh, I know it's a long shot, but I have already researched the cryogenic preservation companies in Southern California, and they are unbelievably expensive. I thought I would look into this as a possible cheaper alternative. You could place me under the Pirates of the Caribbean ride I've been working on."

A stunned Roy turned and said to the man sitting next to him, "Mr. Fanucci, thank you for your time, but I think this is something my brother and I should discuss further in private. If you could show yourself out."

As the man gathered his papers, relieved and happy to be sent on his way, Walt Disney pressed the intercom button and said, "Dolly, could you please call for the nearest Snow White and have her give a personal tour of the park to Mr. Funicello?"

"Certainly, Mr. Disney."

"We'll be in touch," Walt said to the man as his brother discretely nodded "no" to the poor, confused appliance salesman.

After the utterly bewildered vendor left the room, Walt stamped out his latest butt, lit a new one, and said, "I don't understand why you are so against this."

"It is unproven science! This is not like wishing upon a star and becoming a real, live boy."

"But we are the Magic Kingdom. That is our job to make animated movies from nothing."

"But not to reanimate people, little brother!" Roy threw up his hands in exasperation. "Besides, I thought you planned on getting cremated. Ashes to ashes, and all that." He then stared at his brother's overflowing ash-tray and added, "But it looks like you're already hallway there."

"But if there is a chance I could come back . . ."

"I'm not talking about this anymore today. We'll discuss it later with your wife and daughters and see what they think about it."

"Oh, very well. But I'm sure they will agree," he mumbled before changing the subject. "So, what do you have for me today?"

Roy opened a folder, looked it over and said, "Things are looking good, as you would imagine."

"Imagination is our business."

"Speaking of freezers, we have a script for a movie based on Hans Christian Anderson's *The Snow Queen.* It revolves around a couple of princesses, one with magical powers, and has an annoying little snowman who comes to life for comical relief."

Walt frowned. "A snowman who comes to life? Sounds too much like Frosty. Pass."

"Okay," he said as he pulled out another script. "I have one about the legendary Chinese princess who disguises herself as a man in the emperor's army and saves all of China. It has an annoying little dragon who comes to life for comical relief."

This time Walt scowled. "A Chinese princess? Why would American audiences want to see that?"

"Very well then." He sorted through more. "I have a Scottish princess whose mother turns into a bear. Another Hans Christian Anderson story about a mermaid princess who wins the love of her life and regains her voice by killing a sea witch."

"No and no."

"All right. I have Pocahontas, the Indian princess who saved John Smith." He then looked through the wall of cigarette smoke in front of his brother's disapproving face.

"What is with all these princesses you keep presenting to me? That will never sell. No one wants to see female heroines saving the day. That is NOT what a princess does. A princess *GETS* saved. That is what built this empire. Don't you have any other projects?"

"Yes, of course," He paused, rummaged through the papers on his lap, and looked up. "Oh, that Stan somebody from Marvel Comics has been sniffing around, pestering us again. He still thinks we should make movies out of some of their comic books."

"Comic books," Walt said with a slight cough. "Why would we lower ourselves to that when there are still so many fairy tales and classic books still out there?"

"He swears they will make us millions."

"That is a definite 'no,'" he said as he emptied out his ashtray into the metal trashcan underneath the Brobdingnagian desk and opened a new carton of cigarettes and a fresh pack. "I do not see the day when studios will ever be doing 'comic book' movies. I would rather remake our past animated films into live-action ones first."

"What do you mean, Walt?"

"Well, let's go through our hits over the years. *Cinderella. Alice in Wonderland. Peter Pan. Lady and the Tramp. 101 Dalmatians. The Sword in the Stone.* Even our upcoming animated move *The Jungle Book*. We can remake all of them with real people . . . or real animals . . . or both."

"But our old movies were classics. Practically flawless. Do you honestly think people would pay a second time to see the same movie?"

'We're Disney," Walt reminded him. "They will love—and even better, BUY, anything we tell them to." He took another drag. "That reminds me." He reached down and pressed the intercom button. "Dolly!"

"Yes, Mr. Disney."

"Dolly, has Kurt Russell arrived yet?"

"Yes, Mr. Disney. He just got here."

“Good. Good. Please send him in.”

He then arose and walked over to the door to great his young star.

“Hello, Mr. Disney,” Kurt said as he entered the room and shook Disney’s hand. “Golly, it sure is nice to be here today, sir.”

He tousled young Kurt’s hair while still holding his cigarette, accidentally getting some ash in it, and then led the boy over to the empty chair before returning to his own as he said, “And you know my brother, Roy.”

Reaching over to shake the elder Disney’s hand, he said, “Gosh, I sure do. What an honor to be here with the both of you important men.”

“Fine. Fine,” Walt said as he settled into his chair and stomped out the latest cigarette butt and lit another. “But I’m afraid I have some news that will affect you.”

“Golly, what is it, Mr. Disney?”

“I’m sure you have heard about what happened with our star, Tommy Kirk.”

“Gosh, yes, Mr. Disney. Everybody has heard. Mari . . . . Mariwane? What’s it called?”

“Marijuana,” his boss informed him in a fatherly manner.

“I can’t really believe it. Is he all right? Has it made him go crazy? I hope he’s not in the hospital.”

“He is fine. It’s kind of you to ask. But as you know, we are a family-friendly studio, and we have had to let him go because of that as well as another reason.”

“Jeepers, that’s a tough break, Mr. Disney. Are you sure there’s nothing we can do for Tommy?”

"I would love to, but there is another reason we have to let him go. A reason even worse than drugs."

"Wow, sir! What could that be?"

Walt looked over to Roy who turned to the young actor and said, "Kurt, have you ever watched gladiator movies?"

A confused Kurt looked at the man speechless.

"What my brother is trying to say, son. Is that, have you ever heard of men who don't like women? That prefer other men."

A wide-eyed Kurt looked the studio boss. "Wowzer. You mean Tommy? He doesn't like girls? Gosh, I've never known any guy who doesn't like girls . . . especially skinny, blonde ditzy ones."

"They are very, very few. But they are out there so always be careful."

"I sure will, Mr. Disney." He then thought a moment. "So what will Tommy do now?"

"I don't know. He could always move to Europe. They are more tolerant of that sort of thing there than we are. I just don't see the United States—especially California—ever accepting that sort of lifestyle."

"He could possibly go to Scotland," Roy interjected. "They wear kilts there."

A confused Kurt looked at both men. "But you said this affects me. How?"

Walt tried to take another drag but coughed momentarily. "Glad you asked. Very perceptive of you. Yes. For many years, Tommy was the face of several of our movies. But he is out now. And we think you would be perfect to take his place. How does that sound?"

"Jeepers, Mr. Disney. That would be swell!"

Walt looked down at his massive desktop at the script for *The Jungle Book* sitting on top of a pile of papers and thought about his earlier conversation with Roy. "Say, Kurt. We have our new movie, *The Jungle Book*, coming out next year hopefully. We're toying with the idea of doing a version with real people and animals. What would you think about putting on a black wig and letting us spray paint you brown." He paused before adding, "It washes off. Don't worry about that."

"Golliwillickers, that sounds like a super-duper idea, Mr. Disney."

Walt looked smugly at his brother who asked, "But Walt, are you sure it is appropriate for a white actor to play the part of someone from another race?"

"Of course! That's what acting is. Pretending to be someone else. Why would anyone have a problem with that?" He then turned back to his new young star. "Say Kurt, can you do an Indian accent?"

"Golly, I sure will give it my best, sir." He then stood up, folded his arms straight out in front of his chest and said in a deep voice, "Me heep big Indian. Me heep big warrior. Hunt buffalo."

The Disney brothers grimaced.

Walt turned to Roy and asked, "Do we still have an accent coach on staff?"

"Um, no," Roy replied. "We fired him after hearing Dick Van Dyke's cockney accent in *Mary Poppins*."

"Oh yeah. Well, good for us." He then paused and looked back at the young teenager. "Okay, we can do without it. The next problem is you probably shouldn't do anymore growing for the next couple of years in case we decide to greenlight this project."

A grinning Russell said, "Yes, sir. I'll do my best."

"That's the spirit, lad. Now, it's a beautiful day, and I know you don't want to be locked up here with a couple of old codgers any longer when you could be outside playing baseball and having a Coke. So, I'll let you go for the day."

"Golly, thanks, Mr. Disney," he replied before turning to Roy. "And you too, Mr. Disney. This sure has been swell."

As he left the office, Walt turned to his brother, crushed another cigarette butt into the ashtray and said, "What a fine young man" before lighting a new one. "Still, keep Ron Howard's phone number handy for when Russell gets too old."

Roy smiled and nodded in agreement.

As the door closed behind him, Kurt leaned back against it and muttered inaudibly to himself, "Damn! How long will I have to keep this shit up?" He then considered the rest of his day and decided that it most definitely would not involve baseball and Coke. Instead, he decided he would head down the road where they was a beach movie shooting and check out some of the bikini babes. Maybe he would even spot Annette Funicello! He then looked over to the matronly secretary who was busy typing and announced, "Jeepers Miss Dolly, you have a nice day. I think I'll go to the public library now and read to some orphans."

Dolly smiled and nodded in agreement as the nice young man continued on his merry way.

17

APOLLO XI

ONE SMALL STEP FOR . . . LINE!

The large, unmarked warehouse deep in the Nevada desert was dark within except for overhead lights illuminating each of five desks, along with a light over a sole desk thirty feet away facing the five. Two gray-suited men sat together at the lone desk with a handful of manila folders in front of them. It, along with the other five, had a single microphone in the middle of the desk. The shorter of the two men peered over his horn-rimmed glasses and looked beyond the five desks into the pitched blackness and nodded his head. Five men, one for each of the facing desks, were led to them and directed to sit down by shadowy figures whose faces could not be made out.

"Gentlemen, thank you for agreeing to meet with us under these most unusual accommodations," the shorter man with glasses said. "I am . . . let's say I am Dr. A, and my colleague here is Dr. B."

The taller, thin man nodded.

"We represent the United States government," he continued. "More specifically, we represent NASA."

"NASA?" a voice from the first desk called out.

"Yes, Mr. Brooks. The National Aeronautics Space . . ."

"I know what NASA is! Your goons made it sound like you were the IRS and there was some sort of serious problem." Others mumbled in agreement from their dimly lit desks.

"My apologies. We could only say so much because of security reasons."

"What in the world—pardon the pun—would NASA want with me?" the man from the fourth desk asked.

"I don't think that counts as a pun," a voice from the first desk said.

"Regardless," Dr. A interrupted. "Mr. Nichols, that is a fair question. And the truth is, we have a problem—a very serious problem. And we are hoping one of you can help."

The man at the second desk leaned forward, tapped the microphone with his index finger, and asked, "How can any of us possibly help NASA with a problem. I can't speak for the others, but I know I am not an engineer or a scientist."

"That is correct, Mr. Eastwood," Dr. B interjected. "But you all have different skills, special skills, shall we say, that NASA is in desperate . . ."

"Um, pardon me. Excuse me. But I was told there would be food here."

"Not right now, Mr. Coppola," Dr. A responded. "Please let us stick to the matter at hand."

"Which is, Dr. A-B? Which is also the name of my proctologist, I might add."

"We're getting to that, Mr. Brooks," Dr. B answered.

Dr. A cleared his throat and then leaned ever so slightly toward his microphone. "As you all know, our first lunar landing, the Apollo 11 mission, is coming up in a couple of months, and we have come to conclusion that it will not be successful. In fact, it would end in catastrophe if we were to attempt it."

"A catastrophe? How do you mean?" the man the man at the fourth desk asked.

"I mean exactly that. A catastrophe, Mr. Coppola." Dr. A responded. "We can't do it. We cannot land the lunar module—the Eagle—onto the moon safely. It always overloads the onboard computer system and sends the ship into a spiral. Our astronauts, Neil Armstrong and Buzz Aldrin, would not survive."

"Buzz?" a voice from the desk called out laughing. "An astronaut named Buzz? We have an Eagle and a Buzz. You're serious?"

"Yes, Mr. Brooks. We are," answered an annoyed Dr. B.

"And there is also the matter of the radiation in space and the fact that we have essentially aluminum foil thick shielding to protect them," Dr. B said. "Gene Cernan, the pilot from the Apollo 10 mission just returned from space and is already starting to grow a third ear on his back."

"The public is going to be very disappointed," the man at the second desk pointed out. "The first man landing on the moon was going to make their day."

"Yes, Mr. Eastwood, it certainly would have." Dr. A then straightened the folders on his desk and cleared his throat. "And that's where you all come in."

"What? Are you seriously asking us to break the bad news to the world?" the man at the third desk inquired.

"No, Mr. Nichols. Quite the opposite, in fact. We would rather the public not know," Dr. A said.

"Not know? I'm confused."

"We have spent billions of dollars on our space program. And millions more on the Apollo project to beat the Russians to the moon. People are starting to get grouchy about the amount we have expended. They think it could have put to better use elsewhere."

"So where do we fit in?" The question came from the fourth desk.

“We are hoping one of you would be able to film a fake moon landing that we can show the world.”

A gasp arose from the opposing desks.

“We have duplicates of all the equipment. The landing craft. The spacesuits. We could turn this warehouse into a replica of the lunar landscape and then have you film Neil and Buzz . . .”

“Buzz,” a voice from the first desk guffaws.

“We then have you film Neil and Buzz,” Dr. A continued. “We will shoot up the unmanned Saturn V and have the real command module loop around the moon a few times while are astronauts are still safely here. Then, when it’s time, we’ll drop our extra command module with the unshaven three of them in it into the Pacific Ocean to be picked up to international acclaim.”

“So you want the five of us to do this for you? What if we refuse?”

“Well, first, Mr. Nichols, we plan to choose only one of you,” Dr. B replied. “Second, we would hope for you to do it out of patriotism and love for your country. Plus, you also will be very well compensated, including some very nice tax breaks on your next movie paycheck. But if that is not enough to convince you, we’ve also been having the CIA keep track of each of you for years and are confident you will keep our little secret.”

“That is frightening!”

“Yes, Mr. Nichols,” Dr. B said calmly with a nod. “It’s meant to be.”

"But also very challenging," a voice from the fifth desk said.

"Yes. It would be," Dr. A agreed.

"Let me get this straight," the man from the fourth desk said. "You want one of us to direct what? A movie? A documentary?"

The two scientists looked at each other before Dr. B said, "Yessss. Kind of a realistic combination of the two. A documentary. A drama."

"A docudrama," Dr. A interjected.

Dr B covered the microphone with his hand and said to his colleague, "Docudrama. Is that a word?"

"It is now." Dr. A then clapped his hands together and announced, "Let us begin then. Shall we?" He then opened the first manila folder and pulled out some papers.

"Mel Brooks. Born Melvin Kaminsky. World War II veteran. Correct, sir?"

"Sir? Who you callin' 'sir'? I work for a living."

"Very good," Dr. A continued. "So you recently directed the film *The Producers* with Zero Mostel and Gene Wilder?"

"Oh, I loved that movie! Especially the song 'Springtime for Hitler,'" Dr. B interjected.

The two scientist then leaned together to sing, *"Springtime for Hitler and Germany. Deutschland is happy and gay."*

Mel suddenly belts out, *"We're marching to a faster pace. Look out. Here comes the master race."*

The embarrassed scientists looked back down their papers before Dr. A continued. “So, Mr. Brooks. What do you think? Do you have any ideas for our little, uh, docudrama?”

“Thoughts? Thoughts? I love it. Buzz. Buzz. Buzz. I love that name! I’ll call up Gene Wilder to play Buzz . . .”

“Uh, no, Mr. Brooks,” Dr. A interrupted. “Neil Armstrong, Buzz Aldrin, and Michael Collins will all be, uh, ‘playing’ themselves.”

“Themselves? Wouldn’t it be better with professional actors who can actually act?”

“Well, yes, to a point. But having the astronauts themselves performing the tasks will lend an air of authenticity to the production,” Dr. B explained. “They already know the lingo and the tasks they will need to perform. Like how to move in those suits to make it look believable and which knobs to turn.” He then hesitated and added, “Also, there are some union issues, like SAG and whatnot to deal with.”

“Sounds a little meshugana to me, but you are a government organization.”

“No idea what that means Mr. Brooks, but please tell us about your vision for this project,” Dr. A prompted him.

“Happy to, boys.” He stood up as his desk, waving his arms as he spoke. “I don’t see this as being a musical with a lot of song-and-dance numbers because the spacesuits would be too bulky on the moon, and there’s no room in the space capsule. But that doesn’t mean we can't add a little spark to the production. I picture Michael Collins, alone up in the command spaceship, looking down at the lunar surface. What does he do? He moons the moon while singing a funny song I will think up! It's a natural."

"Um, I'm not sure about mooning the moon, Mr. Brooks," Dr. A said in horror. "I don't think Mr. and Mrs. Middle America is quite ready for that."

"Very well. I got another one. This time, they all three are still in their command spaceship thingy. They each have a tube of their food that they have to eat on these trips. But these tubes just happen to all be baked beans. In a matter of no time, all three of them are breaking wind in that tiny space. Buzz is soon calling down to Houston complaining that they all have had too many beans and begging to be let out in a spacewalk."

"Yessss, Mr. Brooks," Doctor A responded hesitantly. "Let's keep that in mind while we move on to the other candidates."

"Not a problem, boys. If you don't want to use it, I'll find room for the bit in a movie down the road."

"Splendid. Splendid," Dr. A said. "Now, moving on." He focused on the occupant of the second desk and took out the corresponding folder. "Clint Eastwood. Born Clinton Eastwood, Jr. Korean War era veteran. Is that correct?"

"I reckon."

Dr. B quickly covered up their microphone to whisper to Dr. A. "Clint Eastwood. You mean the actor? *Rawhide.*

A Fistful of Dollars, Where Eagles Dare? I don't understand. I thought we were looking only for directors."

"We are," Dr. A whispered. "But I hear he is looking to become a director as well someday. So I thought, if the others don't work out, perhaps we hire him on the cheap to direct this."

"Excellent idea. Plus, *The Good, The Bad, and The Ugly* is maybe my favorite movie of all time. The theme song too."

Together they whispered, "*Wah, wah, wah*," quoting the movie's famous song.

"Are you punks singing the '*wah, wah, wah*' song?"

Dr. A uncovered the mic and both men sheepishly said in unison, "Yes."

"You are considering to hire me for this job? You've got to ask yourself one question: 'Do I feel lucky?' Well, do you, punks?"

"Uh, well, I don't really know how to respond to that, Mr. Eastwood." Dr. A shuffled his papers before him to regain his calm. "So, um, can you, uh, would you, do you think you could give us your thoughts on this project and what you think we should do?"

Eastwood pulled out a tiny cigar from his pocket and lit it. He shook out the match and dropped it to the floor. "First off, a man's got to know his limitations."

Both scientists nodded.

"I don't like the idea of shooting here. It's too close to the American press. Something could leak out. First thing I would do is pack everything up and ship it to Italy and film there. I know people who can help."

Dr. A responded, although he did not want to. "Yes, well, if we had lots of time and an unlimited budget, that would possibly be fine. But we are on tight schedule, and the cost of moving the production site is prohibitive."

"We can offer you all the Tang you can drink for the rest of your life, if that helps," Dr. B tossed in.

The actor took one last draw on his cigar before dropping it down by his foot, where he crushed it into the ground. "Tang, huh?"

"Yes, sir," Dr. B replied.

"Tang's a lot," the movie star answered.

"Um, it can be," Dr. B agreed. "If you drink a great deal of it."

"No. That's a joke. 'Tang's a lot.' Thanks a lot."

"Oooooh," they both said before Dr. A tried to pull them out of the awkwardness. "Very funny, Mr. Eastwood. I don't know why you don't do more comedies."

"I do!" Mel Brooks called out from the first desk.

"Go ahead, Brooks. Make my day" Eastwood said menacingly in the direction of the first desk.

"Gentlemen, please," Dr. A interrupted. He then covered the microphone again and whispered to Dr. B, "Okay, I like him as an actor, but he kinds of scares me. Let's move on."

"Agreed," the other scientist responded. "Besides, the man is just a cowboy actor. He obviously will never ever succeed as a Hollywood director."

"Okay, Mr. Eastwood. We need to move on to the others. We'll have our people call your people." He then turned his attention to the middle desk. "Mike Nichols. Born Mikhail Igor Peschkowsky."

Dr. B quickly covered the microphone. "Pechkowsky? He's Russian?"

"Yes, well, his family was. He was born in Berlin," Dr. A answered.

"Berlin? Berlin? And Russian?"

"It's fine," Dr. A attempted to calm his colleague. "He's Jewish. Came here as a young boy to escape the Nazis. He's as American and lox and bagels."

"Well, if you say so." And he removed his hand from the mic.

"Welcome, Mr. Nichols. And thank you for coming." Dr. A shuffled papers until he found the ones he was looking for. "Soooo, you directed *Who's Afraid of Virginia Wolfe* and *The Graduate*. Is that correct?"

A confused-looking Mike Nichols stared back at them and said, "Yes, but I am puzzled as to why I am here. This is not the type of film I usually work on."

Dr. A peered over his papers to the dapper man before him and said, "Well, you have special skills that we appreciate. You directed Richard Burton and Elizabeth Taylor. The two biggest stars in the world. That must have been very intimidating."

"Yes, it was," Nichols agreed. "They often threw things at me. I still have a dent in my forehead from a large ring Liz took off and hurled at me."

"Yet, you did it. And you came out with a very impressive film. And recently you did *The Graduate* and won the Academy Award for best director. Congratulations on that, by the way. And we figure that anyone who can direct Dustin Hoffman is capable of handling just about any daunting project." Dr. A lowered his papers to watch Nichols nod in agreement. "So what are your thoughts about our docudrama?"

"Well, certainly we want to identify with the angst of the performers. . ."

"Astronauts," Dr. A interrupted.

"Astronauts. Yes. Sorry. Their fears. Their struggles. We want every person around the world to care about them and whether or not they will survive."

Dr. B's eyebrows raised. "Exactly."

"That's why I think, just like in *The Graduate*, the soundtrack will be very important.

"Excuse me? Did you say 'soundtrack'?"

"Yes. I would love to use Simon and Garfunkel again but . . ." He leaned over to get nearer to his microphone and said in a hushed voice, "I hear they are not getting along very well and are very close to breaking up."

"Noooo," Dr. B responded as he put his elbow on the table and rested his chin on his hand. "Really? But they seemed so happy and successful."

"It's true! I hear that . . ."

"Gentlemen, we are getting sidetracked here," Dr. A again interrupted.

"Anyway," Nichols continued. "I propose we get the Bee Gees. They are up and comers. Very popular. Plus, they are family, so less likely to break up. I see us using a new music genre that I am inventing: one of dance music based on the urban nightlife scene. Its sound will be recognized by four-on-the-floor beats, electric piano, synthesizers, syncopated basslines, string sections, horns, and electric rhythm guitars. And I shall have them perform a song I will write that will relate to the struggles the astronauts are going through. They lyrics will be something like, 'Staying alive. Staying alive. Yeah. Yeah. Yeah. Yeah. Staying alive.' The audience will care about the men on the moon, and they will have a snappy song they can dance to."

"It's no 'Springtime for Hitler!'" a voice yelled out from the first desk.

"I'm sorry, Mr. Nichols," Dr. A said. "There is not going to be soundtrack. We want people to think this is really happening."

"Why can't there be a soundtrack? Who says there cannot be a soundtrack?"

"*I* say so, Mr. Nichols," Dr. A sternly replied.

"Oh, and I supposed you represent all of NASA on this?"

"Yes. Yes, I do."

Crossing his arms, Mike Nichols took a deep breath, looked upward to the left, and then upward to the right where he continued staring while scowling.

"Mr. Nichols?" Dr. A called out. "Mr. Nichols?"

No response.

Dr. A then covered the microphone with his hand and whispered to Dr. B, "Is he pouting?"

"I believe he is."

Letting out a deep breath, Dr. A removed his hand from the microphone, picked up a different folder, opened it, and looked in the direction of desk four. "Very well then. Francis Ford Coppola. Born Francis Ford Coppola in Detroit, Michigan."

"Present," Coppola called out. "Again, I was told there would be refreshments here. I wasn't looking for anything big, maybe just some canapés, a few antipasto kababs, perhaps some zucchini fritters with a Coca-Cola to wash them down with."

"Francis Ford Coppola?" Dr. B whispered to Dr. A.

"He directed *Finian's Rainbow* with Fred Astaire and Petula Clark." Dr. A responded.

"*Finian's Rainbow*? That pile of crap?" Dr. B whispered loudly. "I mean, I love Fred Astaire and Petula Clark, but that thing was abysmal."

"Agreed," Dr. A said. "My wife and I walked out of the theater halfway though and . . ."

"Sirs," Coppola called out. "You forgot to cover the mic. I can hear every word you are saying."

"Sorry."

"Sorry."

Dr. A then reshuffled his papers and asked, "So, Mr. Coppola. You have heard what your colleagues have had to say so far. What are your thoughts on our lunar docu-drama project?

"I'm sorry. I haven't really been paying attention. My stomach has been growling this entire time. I mean, would it have been so hard to have at least a salad bar out. Maybe a few cannolis to nosh on? I mean, you've already spent billions on your lunar toys. Couldn't you have hidden another hundred in some budget line and gotten one lousy, stinking food truck here?"

Dr. A leaned over to Dr. B and said, "Okay, I don't think this guy is going to work out."

"I agree," Dr. B. answered. "I can't see him ever directing anything successful in his career."

"Again, sirs," Coppola called out. "You forgot to cover the mic, and I can still hear every word you are saying."

"Sorry."

"Sorry."

Dr. A covered the mic and said, "So now what? So far, none of these have sounded impressive. This last director would be perfect. But he's been so successful, I can't imagine him be willing to do our project. Anyone else on your radar before we talk to the last one?"

"There is a recent film student graduate his professors are impressed by. His name is George Lucas. We could give him a call."

"A film student graduate?" Dr. A. sneered. "I can go to any local McDonald's and find a half dozen of those working there."

"Very well. We'll move on to our final candidate."

Dr. A removed his hand from the microphone and said, "Mr. Kubrick? Born Stanley Kubrick. Currently living in Great Britain."

"Yes."

"And have you been listening to everything that has been said about the production so far?" Dr. A asked.

"Yes."

"Groovy," Dr. B. said.

Dr. A looked inquisitively at his colleague.

Dr. B covered the microphone with his hand and whispered, "It is 1969. These are show business folk. I am just trying to make a connection with him."

Dr. A nodded, and after Dr. B removed his hand, leaned into the microphone and said, "Groovy."

"You have a most impressive list of credits" Dr. A. continued. "*Paths of Glory. Dr. Strangelove*, and of course, my personal favorite: *Spartacus*."

"I am Spartacus!"

"I am Spartacus!"

"I am Spartacus!"

"No, I am Spartacus!" the voices from the other desks rang out.

"Very original, guys!" Kubrick called out. "It's not like I don't hear that one about a dozen times each day."

Muffled giggling could be heard from the other four desks.

"But the movie we most wish to discuss is your last one," Dr. A said. "*2001: A Space Odyssey*. This, I believe, is exactly what we are looking for."

"I'll do it."

"Experience with lunar landscapes. Great cinematography," Dr. A read off from his list.

"I'll do it."

"Excuse me?"

"I said I'll do it."

"Wait. So, no problems lying to the public about the moon landing? No moral conundrums?"

"Nope. I'll do it."

"Well," a surprised Dr. B said. "That's wonderful. So, you've heard the comments by the other potential directors here. You're not asking for theme music? To moon the moon? A food truck. Tang?"

"No, I'll do it."

"Wow. That is great. Thank you so much," Dr. A said as he nodded to the darkness behind the desks. Silently, four shadowy figures came up behind the men sitting at desk one to four and stuck a needle into each of their necks, causing them to pass out, where they were each picked up by the armpits by the figures and dragged away into the blackness.

Stanley Kubrick looked down at what was happening next to him and coldly asked, "Are they all right?"

"Yes," Dr. A replied. "They will be fine. But they will have no memory of what happened here today. They will simply wake up, confused, missing a day out of their lives."

Kubrick nodded.

"If I may ask, Mr. Kubrick?" Dr. B spoke up. "Why? We know you have no great love of the country of your birth, which is why you moved overseas. So why are you doing this for us?

Shrugging, the enigmatic Kubrick said, "I like a challenge. To pull off a hoax such as this would be the greatest cinemagraphic challenge of all time." He then nodded his head toward the now-empty desks. "Will that happen to me when it is all said and done?"

"No. No. Of course not," answered Dr. A. "We want you to see the fruits of your efforts. We trust you implicitly."

"Good. Because I now have thought of a small request I would like to include."

"A small request."

"Very small. Hardly worth mentioning."

"Very well, Mr. Kubrick. What is it?"

"The monolith they found on the moon in 2001. I would like for that to be in a background shot on the lunar surface behind the astronauts at some point. I feel it would tie the two projects together nicely,"

"I agree," Dr. A said. "Consider it done."

Dr. B gave his fellow scientist as quizzical look and covered the microphone. "What are you doing? There is no way we can have that black monolith in the moon landing."

"Don't worry," whispered Dr. A. "We film two weeks before the actual takeoff. We can just edit it out in postproduction before giving Mr. Kubrick his shot in the neck."

Dr. B took his hand off the microphone and said, "Very well, Mr. Kubrick. We look forward to working with you. Of course, in return, we will need you to let us in on the little mystery of what that monolith represented in your *2001* movie. Everyone has theories."

"I can only tell you what the aliens told me," the director mumbled under his breath. "I can only tell you what the aliens told me."

18

ELIZABETH II

BLOWIN' IN THE WIND

In almost a military march, Prince Philip strode purposely to the elevator, pressed the button, and stepped in, when he heard a voice call out, "Hold it! Hold the lift, please!" And he saw his wife hurriedly coming toward him as he held out his arm to prevent the door from closing.

"Oh, bloody great. One hundred lifts in Buckingham Palace and I'm stuck with her, forced to make small talk," he thought to himself. "At least it's only a couple of floors. And at least she doesn't have the damned corgis with her yapping and jumping about."

"Thank you, dear," her Royal Highness said as she stepped in.

"You're quite welcome, dear," he replied smiling as best he could, stiff upper lip and all that.

He had just started to let loose of the door when he hear another voice call out, "Hold the lift, please! Wait for me, please!" And they both looked down the hallway to see their gangly son Charles running as quickly as he could to them.

"Should I let it close?" the Duke of Edinburgh asked his wife.

"I want to say yes, but he is our son. Keep it open," she mumbled.

An out-of-breath Charles, the Prince of Wales, heir to the throne, rushed into the lift to join them.

"Thank you so much, Mumsy. Thank you, Daddy. Going down?"

"Charles," his mother responded with a nod as he settled in slightly behind her to her right.

"My boy," his father, to the left of his wife and slightly behind her as well after he let go of the door, taking one last look to make sure no one else wanted a ride.

"You don't have the little blighters with you today?" Charles asked.

"No, they are currently being wormed," his mother responded.

"Oh, I was talking about my younger brothers."

Philip chuckled while his wife remained stoic and said, "Probably would be a good thing for them as well."

No sooner had the words left his mouth when suddenly the lift shook and stopped.

"I say," her Royal Highness said as she reached out to her husband and son to steady herself and keep from falling. "That is not supposed to happen, I believe."

"I should say not, Mumsy," Charles agreed indignantly. "One hundred lifts in this building and we happen to all get in the one that is all caddywhompus."

His mother looked back-and-forth around the space and asked, "Well, what should we do? We are trapped here."

Charles pointed to a little door in the wall by the sliding doors. "I believe there is a phone there for you to call in just such an occurrence."

The queen opened the little door and saw the phone receiver. Turning, she smiled at her son, "Ah, well done, Charles. You would make a fine commoner, knowing these sorts of things."

Charles beamed back, although he was not quite sure if she had meant her statement as a compliment or a slight.

She then pulled the receiver to her ear and said, "Hello." She waited a second. "Hello?" She waited a few seconds more. "Hello? Is anyone there? This is your sovereign speaking."

She then looked back and said, "There doesn't seem to be anyone there."

Prince Philip rolled his eyes and said, "Oh, give me that." He then put it to his ear. "I don't hear a ring tone or anything." He then tapped it in his the palm of his hand a couple of times while the queen and her son gave each other a quick, knowing glance before he put the receiver back up to his ear and yelled, "Hello! Is anyone bloody well out there?"

"Philip!" his wife chided him. "Language."

"Well that was useless," he said as he hung the phone back up in its cradle. "Damn thing was probably installed by your great-great grandmother, Victoria, a century ago."

A few seconds later, they heard a voice call out from above, "Allo! Allo! Anybody stuck down there?"

"Oh. Oh. Thank goodness," Elizabeth said. She then tilted her head up and screamed as loud as a sixteenth-century fishmonger, "Yes. Yes, we are. The phone doesn't seem to be working, and we are indeed stuck down here."

"And 'o might it be that is stuck, if I may ask?"

"It is I, the queen, Elizabeth." And then she added for emphasis, "Your boss!"

"Blimey," came the response. "Sorry, your royalness. I'll get spit spot on the blower to the lift repairman. He should be over right away."

Elizabeth turned to her husband and son with a quizzical look. "Blower?"

"Telephone, Mumsy."

"Ah, quite right. Quite right." She then called up. "Very well! Get right on it, my good man! Oh, and your name?"

"Ferguson, your royalness. I'm on my way to make the call."

"Oh god," Philip said annoyed. "A Scotsman."

A couple of minutes later, the man's voice called down, "I just got done talking to the repairman. He said he will be here in a couple of hours."

"A couple of hours?" the incredulous woman called up.

"Yes, your queenship. Said he's got a couple of stops to work on their broken lifts before this. Then he'll be here to work on ours."

A couple of stops? But I am your queen. Your monarch."

"Yes, mum. I told him that."

"And he said?"

"He said, 'Well, I didn't vote for her.' That's what he said."

"Vote for me? You don't vote for your monarch. I am ordained by God to be your sovereign." She then mumbled, "Or something like that."

She looked at Philip who said, "Yes, I've always been a little fuzzy about the reason myself."

Charles shrugged and mumbled, "Just so long as I remain first in line of succession. I don't care who ordains it. It could be Dr. Who for all I care."

"Isn't there someone else you can call?" Elizabeth yelled up.

"Well, this is the fellar we usually use. He's the cheapest. I can look up in the phone book and see if anyone else can maker down 'ere."

"You do that! Money is no object! I repeat, money is not an object!"

And again, silence followed as they hoped he had done as his queen commanded.

"I miss the days when a monarch could have someone like a lowly repairman drawn and quartered for insolence," Elizabeth said to her fellow stranded companions. "Didn't vote for me, indeed."

"A bit over the top, don't you think, Mumsy?"

"Perhaps we could re-open the prison in the Tower of London and have him sent there."

"Splendid idea, Philip." She then added, "And perhaps, if it ever becomes fashionable again, we could have him burned at the stake."

They then all laughed at the thought of the unknown lift repairman screaming for mercy as flames licked up his body and slowly consumed him in an agonizing, horrific death.

Elizabeth sighed and resignedly said, "So, it looks like we are all going to be here for a while. Charles, get down on all fours so your mother can have a place to sit."

He and Philip stared at her with wide eyes before Charles said, "Mumsy, are you joking?"

"Certainly not. I am tired, and I would rather not sit on the dirty floor. Do you know how many of our staff use this lift each day? It probably has more germs down there than the floor of a Great War trench."

"Be reasonable, Dear," Philip interjected. "The boy couldn't possibly hold you."

The queen turned with a vicious fury, her eyes lit in anger. "What? Are you saying I'm too fat for him to hold me?"

"No. No. No." Philip quickly responded. "The exact opposite. Charles is too skinny. I mean, just look at him."

They both turned at looked up and down at their thin, confused son.

"I mean, the young man probably couldn't hold a tit bird on his emaciated back without collapsing," his father said in his eldest son's defense.

"Oh, very well. I shall stand," she said. "At least until I crumple in a heap." But she still glared unhappily at her eldest son.

Eager to change the topic, Philip said, "So, Charles. Tell us about this young, blonde woman you are currently seeing. Deidre. Is that her name?"

Relieved to have the subject changed, Charles enthusiastically said, "Diana."

"Diana," his mother said. "And she is not a commoner?"

"No, Mumsy," he replied, "In fact, her family has more royal blood than do we."

"Oh." She was not amused.

"I noticed she is taller than are you," Philip said. "Never marry a woman taller than yourself. They start getting pushy in the long run, always wanting attention, always wanting their way."

"Diana is not like that, I assure you. She wants nothing but to stay quietly in the background."

"Yes, always marry a short, petite woman, I always say. Right dear?" he added, looking at his wife. "You'll be much happier."

His wife smiled at the implied compliment that she is petite, which was most certainly better than being thought of as too fat for her son to hold her weight.

Without warning, a dreadful smell filled the lift. Both men looked at Elizabeth and frowned. The queen, knowing it had not been her, turned to both of them and said, "It was not me."

"It's quite all right, Mumsy. It is a natural biological act."

"Yes, dear. Everyone breaks wind from time to time—even queens."

"I assure you, it was NOT me!" she said, getting more irate.

Philip leaned toward Charles and whispered in his ear, "Usually she has the corgis with her to blame when this sort of thing happens."

"Or Andrew or Edward," Charles replied with a grin.

"Not like your sister, Anne," Philip said. "She just lifts a leg and lets it rip. She can clear a room in a second and seems proud to do so."

She glared at them and was about to say something in retort when the lift lurched and started to go down again. The doors opened for them to find a smiling, red-headed, middle-aged man grinning at them.

"We fixed 'er, your royalness," he said before looking at Philip and Charles. "Oh, my pardon. I didn't know there were others stuck in there with ya. Are they important too?"

They disembarked from the lift as the queen said to the man. "Well done, Mr. Ferguson. So you were able to get a repairman here after all."

"Oh, no your queenship. Twarn't able to do that. I just went down and ended up finding the problem meself. It turns out there was a dead rat underneath stuck in the pulleys. Once I pulled the little bugger out, everything was right as rain again."

"I see. A dead rat. Well, thank you for your help, Mr. Ferguson." She turned and said to her husband and son. "A dead rat. That was probably what created that awful smell."

She then turned and went on her way down the hallway as Philip and Charles looked at each other with wry smiles before continuing on with their day.

19

MARCEL MARCEAU

THE ART OF SILENCE

The young reporter looked himself over to make sure he was presentable for the most important interview of his fledgling career—an interview with the greatest mimist of all time. *Wait! Is it mimist? Mimer? Mummer, I believe is correct but sounds really silly. Perhaps it is just "mime." I wish I had looked it up before traveling all the way to Paris.* He then placed his writing pad and pencil in his left hand and straightened his hair and cupped his hand and checked his breath before ringing the buzzer of the apartment with his right.

"Monsieur Marceau?" he asked, although he knew perfectly well who was standing before him, even though the gentleman was not wearing his trademark makeup and costume.

"Ah, oui, you must be the writer from the American magazine. Come in. Come in. You sit there on the divan, and I shall sit across from you on the settee. I hope the sun is not in your eyes. I like the sun. Don't you? But who doesn't. Vampires, I imagine. I suppose the best place to start is the beginning. My beginning. Of course, I was not born Marcel Marceau. I was born Marcel Mangel. My older brother, Alain, and I adopted the name 'Marceau' during the Nazi occupation during World War II. We did so to honor the French Revolution Général François Séverin Marceau-Desgraviers. But more about that later. I was born in Strasbourg, France on March 22, 1923. My father was a kosher butcher named Charles Mangel. I love kosher food. He was originally from Będzin, Poland. My mother, Anne Werzberg, came from what is today the Ukraine. But I know you are less concerned about that than you are my career and what shaped me to become a world-famous mummer, mime, mimest, whatever. And how I created my most famous character, Bip the Clown. I like the color blue very much. Have I told you that yet? It is probably not important. Forget that I mentioned it. Well, it started when I was a young boy of five and mother took me to see a Charlie Chaplin film, which enthralled me and made me want to become a mime, a mimest, or mummer or whatever. But, c'est la guerre, the Nazis would come goose stepping into Paris within a few short years and changing our lives forever.

Because I am Jewish, of course my life was immediately in danger. So my brother and I went to Limoges and joined the French Resistance. We helped many many Jewish children escape to Switzerland. A lovely country. Alps. Julie Andrews singing. And I was able to use my performance skills to help keep them quiet and happy on the journey. The children, I mean, not Julie Andrews. Gloriously, Paris was liberated—no thanks to Coco Chanel, who sold out her own people so she could have a bigger apartment in a fancy hotel during the war. But I soon gave my first major performance in August of 1944 to 3,000 soldiers. My brother and I joined the French Army for the remainder of the war. I then worked as a liaison officer with General George Patton's Third Army because I speak English, German, and French fluently. General Patton was as loud as I was silent, I soon found out. And please do not worry about Parisians hating you and being rude. They are not like that to just Americans but to anyone who is not Parisian—including other Frenchmen. In 1947, I created my Bip the Clown character who wore a striped pullover shirt and a saggy, droopy-flowered silk opera hat. It is a lovely day out today. Don't you think? I love lovely days. But back to the matter at hand. People ask me what it is about Bip, and I tell them, 'Bip is the romantic and burlesque hero for our time. Bip is a modern-day Don Quixote.' As you probably know, I refer to miming as the 'Art of Silence.' Music and silence combine strongly because music is done with silence, and silence is full of music. Music conveys moods and images. Even in opera, where plots deal with the structure of destiny, it's music, not words, that provides power. Mime is an art beyond words. It is the art of the essential. And you cannot lie. You have to show the truth. Do not the most moving moments of our lives find us without words? The great problem of humanity is life and death, which has absolutely nothing to do with what I am talking about here, so just forget I said anything about. I am a company in myself. That is why in 1949 I founded the Compagnie de Mime Marcel Marceau. My repertoire has become a bible for all mimes or mummers or mimests in the world. I became a huge hit in France, which some would say does not mean a lot considering our adoration of your Jerry Lewis, but trust me, I was a really big deal. So big that I had an affair with Marilyn Monroe. Don't believe all that nonsense about her and John F. Kennedy and Bobby Kennedy. And do not get me started about her and Albert Einstein. Albert completely made all of that up to impress people and also to distract them from some of his professional setbacks in my opinion. He had a Brobdingnagian imagination. But no, I attained her affection by miming that I was trapped in a glass box and then breaking through it to present her my heart. She was so impressed, I won her for my own. She eventually left me. I tried to throw an invisible rope around her to pull her back, but it did not work. C'est la vie. Still, I had great success in America other than just with movie starlets. I won one of your Emmys. I was on the *Dinah Shore Show, The Mike*

Douglas Show, The Red Skelton Show, and your *Laugh-In*. I was even in the Mel Brooks film *Silent Movie*. But I will never work with the man again. Monsieur Brooks knows nothing about writing good dialog. I have performed L'art du silence around to world. I have been stuck inside so many invisible boxes and had so many invisible flowers droop that I have lost count. Did I mention that I hated Charles DeGaulle. Probably not important. Don't know why I mentioned it. But I do apologize. I am going on and on. Never get a mime, mimest, mummer or whatever talking. He won't stop. Do you have any questions so far?"

"Um, yes, Monsieur Marceau. I'm sorry. My pencil broke when you started speaking. Would you mind repeating it?"

20

BILL C

IS PMS BIBLICAL?

Mankind has survived the Dark Ages, enjoyed the Renaissance Age, delved into the Age of Enlightenment, plodded through the Post-Christian Age until, at last, it has arrived at where it stands now -- the Age of Oprah (also known as the "Age of Confusion").

In all other ages except the current one, the Christian male always knew where he stood. He was the head of his household and king of his domain. If his wife disagreed about something, he could simply quote Ephesians 5:22 ("Wives submit yourself to your husband . . .) and the matter would be settled. But roles are no longer so clear-cut. With that ambiguity has come confusion, and with that confusion has come problems within the home.

At Hosea House, they are working to help Christian men deal with these problems. Named after the cuckolded minor prophet of the Old Testament who was married to a tramp, Hosea House is a men's shelter originally established to give husbands whose wives suffer from severe premenstrual symptom (PMS) a place to escape to for a couple of days each month if conditions at home became potentially too dangerous.

"Thirty years ago PMS seemingly didn't exist," says Bob D. (Most names in this article have been changed to protect the anonymity of all concerned.) "Before, women suffered silently. Now however, they don't, and they're out with a vengeance."

Bob D. continued to explain that no one knows the exact reasons why this has changed. Some blame Oprah Winfrey. Others believe it is the fluoride in the water or nanobots in vaccines. Whatever the reason, it does not change the fact that there are men out there who need help.

Take the case of Bill C., a former high-ranking member of the executive branch in the federal government, who has been coming to the shelter for three days each month for the past five months.

"The first time I saw the hotline number was while smoking a cigar and reading the sports page one day," he tells us. "I never had the nerve to call until one evening when I came home an hour late from a uh, public engagement, because of the traffic. I had just walked in the door and called out to H., my wife, in the kitchen and asked her what was for supper. The next thing I knew, she was running into the living room and pelting me with burnt meatballs. I called the hotline from my cellphone from inside my car in the driveway of my house immediately."

That night Bill C. was safe and secure in Hosea House. Today he is in counseling and a support group to help him deal with his dilemma.

At Hosea House they know that providing shelter is not enough. They need to provide a nurturing environment, and that is where the counseling and support groups enter the process. The residents are encouraged to take classes such as: *Why That Extra Y Chromosome Does What It Does*; *Manly Men of the Bible: a Study of Joshua, Samson, and Peter*; *Is PMS Biblical?*; and *Give Me That Old Time Chauvinist Religion*.

"In addition, we encourage the men to watch old Charlton Heston movies, especially *The Ten Commandments* and *Ben Hur*," adds Bob D. "The use of positive role models who are virile Christian men is always stressed. Well, even though the men he plays in these movies are technically Jewish. But you know what I mean."

As for the support groups, Bill C. says, "At first, I wanted to hide what happened to me. After all, I once had my finger on the nuclear button . . . I mean, I once was a powerful man. Then I realized that it was okay.

These guys are as whipped as I am. They know what I'm going through."

In the support groups, an atmosphere of traditional Christian male bonding is fostered. Members are discouraged from "getting in touch with their feminine sides." They may talk about their "situation" but are not allowed to elaborate further on their feelings. Hugs are forbidden and firm masculine handshakes are practiced. Sports must be talked about for at least half of every session, and support groups are scheduled so as never ever to conflict with Monday Night Football.

"I've learned that just because I don't suffer from PMS or go through the pain of childbirth, that does not legitimize her anger being directed toward me," Bill C. says.

At Hosea House, the men are taught that, despite the classes and the counseling sessions, they are never completely through. There will be setbacks in their lives. There will still be those occasional months where their Christian right of headship is ridiculed, beaten to a pulp, and left sitting out in the garbage with the previous night's discarded leftovers. They must not be daunted by these reversals but must stand tall and say to their wives, "I am a Christian and I am a man. You diminish yourself when you behave thusly toward me."

If they're still conscious and standing after that remark, then they have regained their Biblical manhood.

As for the future of Hosea House, Bob D. explains that money is always a problem. "There is a tremendous necessity for so many more shelters nationwide and funding never keeps pace with demands. However, we are hoping to expand soon to include long-term shelter for husbands whose wives are moody and hormonal due to pregnancy. One client, Bill C., says he has a foundation with tons of money just sitting around and has promised to help."

"It's the least I can do, and we do try to do the least we can do," Bill C. attested.

Some people do street-corner evangelism, others run Christian daycare centers, but at Hosea House they recognize the needs of the forgotten Christian male and are working to meet those needs. They dream of the day when Hosea Houses will not be required, and Christian men may enter into a new era -- the Age of Heston.

21

BARACK OBAMA

KENYA BE PRESIDENT

As he paced the floor of his home, Senator Barack Obama threw up his hands in frustration as he looked at his wife, Michelle, and said, "It is so frustrating. I know I can help this country. It's such a stupid rule!"

Michelle nodded and rubbed his back as she tried to calm him down. "I know. I know. But are you sure you were born in Hawaii and not Kenya?"

"Yes! No. I don't know. I was just a baby at the time," he replied. "One relative says one thing. Another says something else. In my heart of hearts, I am Hawaiian."

"Mahalo, dear."

"It's just such a ridiculous rule. Why would we have such a requirement to stand in my way."

Young Malia looked up from her seat at the dining room table where she was playing Scrabble and said, "Actually, Father, there has been precedent as to why such a rule has been emplaced by many countries throughout history. After all, Alexander the Great was not actually Greek but Macedonian. Napoléon Bonaparte was not French but Corsican. Josef Stalin was from Gori, now known as Georgia, and not Russia. Adolf Hitler was Austrian and not German. And Ryan Reynolds is not American but Canadian."

Barrack and Michelle stared at each other in amazement before his wife said, "Wow, chalk one up for the mediocre Illinois educational system."

Malia looked back down to concentrate on the letters from her game.

"Still, I have so many ideas, so many actions I wish to take to move this country back to its rightful level with the other countries in the world. For instance, we are a generous and welcoming people, but those who enter our country illegally, and those who employ them, disrespect the rule of law. And because we live in an age where terrorists are challenging our borders, we simply cannot allow people to pour into the U.S. undetected, undocumented and unchecked. Americans are right to demand better border security and better enforcement of the immigration laws."

"You might want to rethink that one before you hit the campaign trail," Michelle suggested.

"Why? It's just common sense, isn't it?" her husband asked. "Bill Clinton agrees with my stance."

"We'll discuss it later."

"What if we can't find a birth certificate? There has to be some way to get around this."

Michelle crossed her arms and looked up at the ceiling as she thought. "Perhaps there is."

"Well, what?"

"We don't confirm or deny it," she said.

Barack threw up his hands. "How will that help?"

"Let me finish, Barry." She then continued. "We won't have to. Look, the internet is now the biggest thing out there. Everyone uses it to get all sorts of information. Some of it accurate. Some of it just plain crazy. I say we use that to our advantage."

"How?"

"We secretly post on message boards and fill them with completely wacko theories on all sorts of things. Because of that, they will be really popular in no time."

"Keep going. What kind of theories?"

"Oh, anything we can come up with to pass on. Others will soon jump online with their own."

"What should we come up with?"

She shrugged. "I don't know. How about that lizard people theory?"

"Lizard people?"

“Yes,” she said. “You know. Aliens are living among us. They are actually lizards, but they have disguised themselves to appear human. And they want to take over the government, planet, blah, blah, blah.”

“You’re joking.”

“I wish I were. It’s crazy, but a good place to start.”

“What else?

“Saying 9/11 was an inside job is another,” she replied. “The moon landings were staged with Stanley Kubrick directing them. Climate change will kill us all in ten years. Vaccines have little nanobots in them that take over our personalities.” She paused. “Oh, and wealthy people around the world are kidnapping children and drinking their blood as an eternal youth elixir.”

“Ewww. And how does it help me get to the presidency?”

“Over time we’ll flood social media with the wildest things we can think of. Then, we’ll add your Kenyan birther theory in as part of it. By that time, the message boards and social media sites repeating these wild claims will be so discredited that we’ll have most of the news media eating out of our hand and laughing the claim away with the others.”

“You really think the mainstream media are that stupid that they will ignore it?”

“Barry, they won’t even look into it. They don’t bother to check anything anymore.”

“Well, then we have to give ourselves a cool nickname. Like “Deep Throat” or “JFK” or something” he suggested.

"Sure," Michelle said as she looked around and then down at Malia's Scrabble board where she spied the letters Q, N, N, A, O. "How about Q?" she offered.

"Sounds a little James Bondish."

"Okay," she sighed. "Then how about . . . QAnon?"

"Sounds good," he said. "And you think all this will be enough to get me the presidency?"

"No," she answered, as she looked him up and down. "There's more we'll need to work on. I mean, I hate to tell you this, but you are Black. That will be a problem for some voters."

"I'm proudly half-white, too," he replied indignantly.

"That probably won't be enough for some crackers, I mean, citizens."

"Well, I can't change how I look."

"No, but we can do other things that will distract them."

"Like what?"

"Well, you'll need to name a vice president."

"Hillary?"

"Oh god, no," she quickly replied. "Remember, she and Bill are the ones who started this whole birther conspiracy nonsense. No, you should find the antithesis to you. Like, some old, handsy, racist white guy who constantly says and does crazy things . . . like a creepy, eccentric uncle. The media and voters will be focusing so much on him that they'll let you slide."

"Like who?"

"I don't know. That covers about half the Democratic Party. Just choose anyone who will make you look good."

"You seem to have given my run for the presidency a great deal of consideration." He paused and added, "Maybe even more thought than I have given it."

"Oh, don't be silly, honey." Michelle laughed and patted him playfully on the top of his head. "Now, it's a nice day. Why don't you grab your basketball and go outside and shoot some hoops."

"Okay, Mom. . . I mean, Michelle."

He started toward the door, then turned and said excitedly, "Oh, I have another one. We could go with the theory that says the Clintons have anyone killed who threatens to expose their criminal activities."

Michelle frowned. "Oh, I'm sorry, honey. We can't use that one. It's true."

"Darn." And with that, he was out the door as he mumbled, "Lizard people. Crazy!"

Michelle turned back to where Malia was playing her game. Just then, a fly alit onto an apple in the fruit bowl in the middle of the table. Simultaneously, long, forked tongues struck out from both their mouths toward the fly, with Malia being the winner of a tasty snack. She looked up at her mother proudly. Michelle smiled in return and then went back to planning her "husband's" presidential campaign.

www.ingramcontent.com/pod-product-compliance
Ingram Content Group UK Ltd.
Pitfield, Milton Keynes, MK11 3LW, UK
UKHW021937190726
13853UKWH00004B/1505